The "Truth"
of the
Matter Is!

By Mary J. Parker

Copyright © 2006 by Mary J. Parker

ISBN 0-7414-2924-1

Published by:

INFI∞ITY
PUBLISHING.COM

1094 New DeHaven Street, Suite 100
West Conshohocken, PA 19428-2713
Info@buybooksontheweb.com
www.buybooksontheweb.com
Toll-free (877) BUY BOOK
Local Phone (610) 941-9999
Fax (610) 941-9959

Printed in the United States of America

Printed on Recycled Paper

Published March 2006

TABLE OF CONTENTS

THE "TRUTH" OF THE MATTER IS!

PREFACE

Fact – A thing said or supposed to be true or to have really happened; anything that is known or alleged to have occurred in connection with a case.

TRUTH – That which is true; matter of circumstance as it really is; fixed or established principle, law, or the like; proven doctrine; the quality or nature of being true, exact, honest, sincere, or loyal.

Our days on earth are filled with "diverse" facts and circumstances that shape our lives. Some facts are positive and some sad to say are negative. We know however, that facts are subject to and often do change. No one knows the total number of people whose lives have been "radically" changed forever based on untrue facts. The same, thank God, cannot be said about **TRUTH!** Truth is just what it is, **TRUTH!** TRUTH *never* changes! It is constant, fixed, and trustworthy because it is **"set in stone."** What stone you ask? This stone is none other than our Lord and Savior **Jesus Christ**! Isaiah 28:16 states: *"Therefore thus says the Lord God, Behold I am laying in Zion for a foundation a Stone, a tested Stone, a precious Cornerstone of sure foundation; he who believes, trusts in, relies on, and adheres to that Stone will not be ashamed or give way or hasten away in sudden panic." (Amplified Bible)* Jesus is the "Chief Cornerstone" rejected of men but made the

i

head of the corner. St. John 14:6 reads: *"Jesus saith unto him, I am the way, the truth, and the life: no man cometh unto the Father, but by me."* The purpose of this book is to encourage people to not just accept the "facts" as they are based on what we see with our "natural eyes." False or misleading ideologies and beliefs can be conceived by our finite and limited "natural" vision. Don't be deceived and fooled. Things are not always what they seem when placed alongside the TRUTH of God's awesome and powerful Word! We must learn to see what TRUTH has to say about the circumstances and situations facing us each and every day. The facts may be the facts, but **_TRUTH_** is always the final **_WORD!_** Remember that it is through God's Word that we are sanctified, for his WORD is TRUTH. TRUTH therefore is the only "voice" we Christians are to live and govern our lives by. In John 16:13 Jesus states: *"Howbeit when he, the Spirit of truth, is come, he will guide you into all truth: for he shall not speak of himself; but whatsoever he shall hear, that shall he speak: and he will show you things to come."* We are not blind to what's taking place in our society. Some of the "facts" that shape our lives on a daily basis are: Unemployment, sickness & disease, poverty, violence, racism, divorce, death of loved ones, depression, confusion, abuse, hopelessness, war, etc. The list seems endless and it does not appear that things are ever going to work themselves out. Those may be the "facts," but ask yourself this question. What is the Truth? Many in our modern and contemporary culture believe that the Bible is outdated and is therefore no longer relevant for today's society. I beg to differ. Not only is the Bible relevant for today, it is more current than our daily newspaper! It is man's instruction book for "life." I pray that the scripture lessons found in this book will better equip you to apply the "Truth of the matter," to the "Facts of your life!"

DEDICATIONS

This book is dedicated with love and appreciation to my Lord and Savior Jesus Christ for saving my soul from hell, and gifting me with these words of inspiration. I thank him for healing me from a two year disability and proving all the doctors wrong who said that I would never use a computer again. To my dear Mother Mary Jones who is one of the best cooks on earth. You are my best friend and number one supporter. Thanks for being a patient, loving, Spirit filled mother. Your sense of humor is what kept me going when the chips were down. Without you, none of this would be possible. You're a shining example to all who meet you of what a Christian should be. There is no one else like you mom. You are the strongest person I know. I love you very much! To my Grandmother Esther Perry whom I love very much. Your faithful witness is what helped me find my way to the house of God. Thanks for being the serious Bible student that you are. Your dedication to study of the scriptures and prayer has inspired me to do the same. You are a strong and courageous woman of Faith. Thanks also for protecting me all those times mom wanted to spank me real good. I truly thank God that you are my grandmother. I couldn't have asked him for a better one! To my Grandfather Randolph Perry, thanks for your prayers and support. Thank you for being a strong man of conviction and not being afraid to speak your mind on certain issues. Thanks most of all for sending me that great tasting country ham and sausage! My Baby Brother Darnell Jones, thanks for all your help through the years. It is because of you purchasing my first computer and assisting me with the upkeep of it, that my gift of writing was even discovered. Thank you for your patience with me over the years. I know I haven't been the easiest person to get along with at times but it was just my way of showing just how much I care for you. Much love to you and your family. To my Great-Aunt Lucille Parker, thanks for being my first babysitter. I had the best time with you and Cousin Matt. You were there for the early years and did a great job looking after me while mom worked. You also were the first person to take me to church. Thank you so much for all you have done for me. I love you and Matthew more than you know. To my wonderful aunts and uncles who were more like older brothers and sisters to me. Thank you for helping my mother raise me and for supporting me in all my endeavors. Thanks especially to Belinda and Helen for sneaking me sweet treats when mom wasn't looking. To the rest of my family, thanks for all you have done and God's greatest blessings to you all! My Pastor Bishop Forbes for preaching the unadulterated Gospel and living the life you preach about before your members. To the warm members at my home Church Faith Temple, thank you for your love, teaching, prayers, and encouragement over the years. To Brother Hayward Waters for giving me the opportunity to write for his newsletter, allowing me to further develop my gift. To Dr. Nathaniel Screven for being the highly anointed teacher that you are. I truly thank God for your school, Evangelical Bible Institute. Sitting under your teaching the last few years has quickened in me an even deeper understanding, yearning, and appreciation for God and his word. Thank you for all your encouragement in regards to this project. To my classmate Big Brother Ronnie C. Enoch who is without a doubt one of the most gifted and highly anointed Christian Poets on earth. Thank you so much for taking me under your "wings" and assisting me with the publication of this book. I couldn't have done it without you. To God be the Glory for you Ron. I'll never be able to repay you for all you have done and are doing for me. Thanks so much! Pastor Chamblee and the sweet members of The Promised Land Baptist Church, thank you for helping me get my zeal and motivation back at a critical time in my spiritual walk. God was taking me to another level in Him and you were there to help me through the transition. My dear friends, thank you for your love, prayers, encouragement and most of all proofreading! You are all the salt of the earth! And last but surely not least, to all the Pastors, ministers, preachers, writers and teachers of the gospel that I have the pleasure of learning from. Continue to sow the word of God. Your labor is not in vain. Your words have grounded themselves in my heart, and with God giving the increase, this is the harvest which has been produced. Isaiah 55:11 states: *"So shall my word be that goeth forth out of my mouth: it shall not return unto me void, but it shall accomplish that which I please, and it shall prosper in the thing whereto I sent it."* This project is proof of that! God has graced me now with the opportunity to do the same for others. And for that, I am eternally grateful. If I've missed anyone, please forgive me. Know that I love you all and pray for God's continued blessings upon your lives.

Foreword

I first met Ms. Parker in Bible School. As I was talking about a book I'd written, she was listening intently. Very quiet and unassuming, this particular day peaked her interest and we began to converse about writing. Little did I realize that she had a book inside her that had to come out. We exchanged phone numbers and the rest is history. I was in total surprise of the material presented to me.

Every now and then God places someone in your life to shake you up so to speak. She's a devout woman of God with such a gift for writing, as you'll see in these pages. You'll find this to be an awesome tribute to the Christ that resides within. So many false teachings today reside in the lukewarm church of this era. People are being moved by what feels good instead of truth, which can sometimes be so difficult to adhere to. The **"The TRUTH Of The Matter Is!,"** is a book that breaks down its components not leaving anything to question. I pray you'd be blessed reading this book as I was.

Ronnie C. Enoch

Chapter 1

"Adversity"

Adversity - A condition of unhappiness, misfortune, distress, calamity, hardship, trouble; being in unfavorable circumstances; need, or sickness (*9)

Fact – Trouble is the one "fact" of life that every one of us will have to deal with and face head on. You don't have to do anything wrong, rest assured, trouble will "find" you. There is no getting around it.

TRUTH – *"We are hedged in (pressed) on every side (troubled and oppressed in every way), but not cramped or crushed; we suffer embarrassments and are perplexed and unable to find a way out, but not driven to despair; We are pursued (persecuted and hard driven), but not deserted (to stand alone); we are struck down to the ground, but never struck out and destroyed." (2nd Corinthians 4:8-9, Amplified Bible)*

"WHEN YOUR CIRCUMSTANCES CHANGE, HOLD TO GOD'S UNCHANGING HAND"

It is easy for us to praise and worship God when things are going well isn't it? The choir seems to sing with the greatest anointing electrifying those in the pews. The sermons that come across the pulpit are the most inspirational ones we have ever heard. Most of all, the Holy Ghost shows up and manifests himself in many through the dance, shouting, crying, and clapping of hands. There is no better place to be on earth than in the service of the Lord! But what happens to our faith when life **suddenly** *"throws us a curve ball"* or *"the bottom falls out?"* What happens to our praise? What I am referring to is when we are faced with a sudden challenge or adversity that changes our circumstances. How do we react? Are we *always* *consistent* in our faith to God or do we sometimes doubt and waver?

I'm sure that **TROUBLE** is the one subject we all can testify about! Trouble comes in all types of forms, sizes, and from all different directions. Job reminds us in chapter 14 verse 1: *"Man that is born of a woman is of few days and full of trouble."(KJV)* Job was a man well qualified to make that assessment. Our lives are filled with circumstances and situations which test our faith and trust in God. Will we be consistent in serving the Lord in spite of what happens? Loss of employment, loss of health, loss of a loved one, divorce, financial woes, your best friend moves out of state, problems with your children, problems in school, drug abuse, alcohol abuse, and oh yes, even problems at the house of God. The list goes on and on. But what do you do when your circumstances *"CHANGE?"* The answer is found in my favorite hymn, **"Hold to God's UNCHANGING Hand."** Don't give up! Don't drop out of the race! Don't throw in the towel! You can make it! Proverbs 3:5-6 states *"Trust in the Lord with all thine heart: and lean not unto thine own understanding. In all thy ways acknowledge him and he shall direct thy paths."(KJV)* I'm striving to do better in this area myself. Let's look to the scriptures and find how others responded when trouble showed up in their lives and suddenly changed their circumstances.

In the first chapter of the book of **RUTH,** we find a woman by the name of Naomi living in the country of Moab. She's living in Moab due to a famine in her homeland Bethlehem-Judah. She lives there with her husband, two sons, and their wives. In the space of ten years, Naomi loses her husband and both of her sons. What an incredible loss. Did she become bitter towards God and give up? No. Chapter 1:6 states *"She arose with her daughter in-laws, that she might return from the country of Moab: for she heard how that the Lord had visited his people in giving them bread." (KJV)* Naomi knew she needed to be where the "people of God" were. Naomi tries to convince her daughter in-laws to stay in Moab, but one, Ruth, chooses to give up her own people and culture to follow Naomi to her homeland. Out of everything Naomi had been through, her life was a powerful witness to the reality of God. Ruth was drawn to her and to the God she worshipped. It is when we are going through our trials and tribulations that the "unsaved" watch us the most. My Pastor Bishop Forbes always tells us *"We are the only Bibles some people will ever read."* Our actions speak louder than words. We demonstrate our belief in Christ by our everyday walk and character. This Old Testament story ends happily. Ruth marries a man named Boaz and becomes the great-grandmother of David, and a descendent in the line of the Messiah. Naomi made a profound impact on Ruth by her life and walk of faith. Naomi despite all she had been through, "held to God's unchanging hand."

Let's look at another example in the Bible of someone who was faced with a challenging situation and how they responded to it. In I Samuel 30:1-6 we find a story about Ruth's grandson, King David. In this passage of scripture, David and his men return to Ziklag only to find that their enemies, the Amalekites, have invaded, smitten, and burned the city with fire. They have taken the women and children captive. When David and his men see that the city has been burned and their families are taken captive, they lift up their voice and weep until they have no more power to weep. As usual, when things go wrong, we look for someone to blame. Verse 6 tells us *"David was greatly distressed; for the people spoke about stoning him."(KJV)* Just think about that for a moment. David went from being a *hero* to a *zero* in the eyes of the people. So how did David respond to this sudden change in his circumstance? The Bible says, *"David encouraged himself in the Lord."(KJV)* This story lets me know that there are going to be times in my spiritual walk with God when no one will be able to hold my hand through certain trials. It is at that moment that I have to **"look to the hills from whence cometh all my help."** Remember, God promised never to leave us alone. "Man" may fail us at times, but God never fails! What happened to the Amalekites you ask? Verses17 -18 read *"And David smote them from the twilight even unto the evening the next day: and there escaped not a man of them, save 400 young men, which rode upon camels, and fled." "And David recovered all that the Amalekites had carried away: and David rescued his two wives."(KJV)*

It is in Matthew the 26th chapter that we find our next example from the Bible. This chapter in Matthew deals with the death and resurrection of Jesus, the King. Verses 31, 33 – 35 states: *"Jesus says unto them, all ye shall be offended because of me this night: for it is written, I will smite the shepherd, and the sheep of the flock shall be scattered abroad." "Peter answered and said unto him, though all men shall be offended because of thee, yet will I never be*

4

offended." "Jesus said unto him, verily I say unto thee, that **this night,** before the cock crow, thou shalt deny me thrice." "Peter said unto him, though I should die with thee, yet will I not deny thee." "Likewise said all the disciples." *(KJV)* Notice that it wasn't just Peter who said this. He was the first one to "speak out" but **all** the disciples said the same thing. After this we see Jesus taking his disciples to the garden of Gethsemane. He takes Peter, James, and John with him while he goes a little farther to pray. Here Jesus wrestles with the "cup." The cup represents his impending trials, betrayal, and death on a cross. He was in great anguish over his coming physical pain, separation from the father, and death for the sins of the world.

Upon completion of his prayer, Judas comes with a great multitude with him wielding swords and staves. Verse 56b says *"then all the disciples forsook him and fled."(KJV)* Do you remember what they said over in verse 35? How would you have responded if you were in their place? Would you have been constant in your faith? In verses 69-74, we find Peter sitting outside the palace where Jesus had been taken. Peter is approached by a girl saying to him, *"thou also was with Jesus of Galilee."* Peter denies it. Later, another girl notices him and tells the people there *"this fellow was also with Jesus of Nazareth."* Peter denies it again, this time with an oath. Lastly, the men who had been standing by came over to Peter and said *"we know you are one of his disciples because your speech gives you away."* *"Then Peter began to curse and to swear saying "I know not the man" and immediately the cock crew."* *"And Peter remembered the word of Jesus, which said unto him "before the cock crow, thou shalt deny me thrice," and he went out and wept bitterly."(KJV)* Can you imagine how Peter must have felt? Have you ever faltered in your faith? I have. Did Peter give up and commit suicide like Judas? Did God give up on him? No. Peter repented and God restored him. God knows that we have to develop our faith. We don't get there overnight. It takes time but hold on to his hand. He will guide you safely through and bring you from faith to faith, and from glory to glory. We may stumble, falter, and sometimes fall but we don't have to stay there. Get up! Repent and ask the Lord to help you. He will. I'm a witness. This same Peter who could not stand up to a little girl, went on to preach one sermon (Acts 2:41) and cause 3,000 souls to be saved.

Our last example of how to respond when your circumstances change comes from Acts 16:22-26. Here we have the account of Paul and Silas being stripped, beaten with many stripes, and put in prison for casting a demon out of a possessed girl. This slave girl made her master rich by fortune telling. Now that the evil spirit had left her, her master's evil way of acquiring personal gain from her unfortunate condition was now gone. Verses 25 & 26 states: *"And at midnight Paul and Silas prayed and sang praises unto God and the prisoners heard them. And suddenly there was a great earthquake, so that the foundations of the prison were shaken: and immediately all the doors were opened, and every one's bands were loosed."(KJV)* That was an awesome prayer meeting! Jesus tells us *"Where two or three are gathered together in my name, there am I in the midst."* Paul and Silas show us that despite what our "physical" limitations might be, there is a freedom in our "spirits" that no chains or fetters could ever confine!

The four examples used in this theme show us that we must hold to God's unchanging hand in spite of what our circumstances are. God is worthy to be praised! There is victory in the Praise! We often sing the song **"Trouble In My Way...I have to Cry Sometimes," but Psalm 30:5b states, *"Weeping may endure for a night but joy cometh in the morning!"*** Remember, when your circumstances change, hold to God's unchanging hand! For he won't let you fall! How can we know this to be true? He makes a promise to us found in Isaiah 41:10. It reads, *"Fear thou* *not: for I am with thee; be not dismayed; for I am thy God: I will strengthen thee; yea, I will help thee; yea, I will uphold thee with the RIGHT HAND of my righteousness."(KJV)* Hold to God's Unchanging Hand!.....

"Time is filled with swift transition,"
"Naught of earth unmoved can stand,"
"Build your hopes on things eternal,"
"Hold to God's unchanging hand!"

(Hymn by Jennie Wilson *6)

Chapter 2

"Afflict/Affliction"

Afflict – To cause pain to; trouble very much; distress: torment, harass, to cast down, dash against. (*9)

Affliction – State of pain, trouble, or distress; misery, wretchedness, tribulation. (*9)

Fact – Affliction, if allowed to, will stop us from succeeding and maximizing the potential that the Lord has given us.

TRUTH – *"Many are the afflictions of the righteous, but the Lord delivereth him out of them all." (Psalm 34:19 KJV)*

TRUTH - *"And the Patriarchs, moved with envy, sold Joseph into Egypt: but God was with him, and delivered him out of all his afflictions, and gave him favor and wisdom in the sight of Pharaoh King of Egypt; and he made him governor over Egypt and all his house." (Acts 7:9-10 Amplified Bible)*

PICKED "ON"
BUT PICKED "OUT"

Have you ever felt like you were the "odd man" out? Were you the last kid picked when the neighborhood children played certain games or sports? Were you often ridiculed and found yourself to be the "butt" of many jokes? You never truly "fit in" no matter how hard you tried. Some may even be dealing with this as an adult. It's not easy being "hen pecked" or considered the "runt of the litter" is it? Only those of us who have experienced or are experiencing this first hand know exactly what I'm talking about. It can be a very hurtful and stressful set of circumstances to have to deal with. We are faced with this challenge in school, work and sometimes even at church. It is for this reason that many of us tend to gravitate to the background. We may feel as though the gifts and talents we possess are "small" and "insignificant" in comparison to what others "seem" to have. We are under the assumption that we can never "measure up" to others so why even try. Jesus tells us *"he who measures himself against another is unwise."* He also tells us to *"be wise as serpents and harmless as doves."* It is good to know however that God cares for you and you are just the type of person He's looking for to use in a mighty way. You may have been or may even be "picked on" but God in His infinite wisdom "picked you out" to be a winner on His side. What do I mean by "picked out?" I mean **chosen**. Jesus tells us, *"with loving kindness have I drawn thee."* I'm so glad He thought enough of me to "pick me out" of the crowd. The Bible tells us *"we were chosen in him before the foundations of the world."* There are many examples in the Bible of those who were "picked on" but "picked out" by God to do extraordinary things.

9

I'm reminded of the story of Noah found in Genesis Chapter 6. Earth was no longer the perfect paradise that God had intended. All of humanity forgot about God except Noah and his family. They were the only people in the world that still worshipped God. Because of Noah's faithfulness and obedience, he is commanded by God to build an ark. God is going to send a vast flood that will destroy every human being on earth. You must keep in mind, at that point in time, there was no such thing as rain on the earth. It took Noah 120 years to build the ark. Can you imagine the public ridicule he and his family must have encountered on a daily basis? The Bible is silent concerning this subject. However, all of us know that "scoffers" are always around those of us who try to uphold and maintain our integrity before the Lord. It is my heartfelt belief their task was met with some opposition. As God would have it, the flood did come and it accomplished that which the Lord said it would. God blessed Noah and his sons and told them to have many children and repopulate the earth. Noah was a man of patience, consistence, and obedience. He was picked "out" to become one of the great heroes of faith in the Bible.

God is in the business of working through his people to accomplish seemingly impossible tasks. Nehemiah was picked "out," prepared, and positioned by God to be used to accomplish one of the Bible's "impossible" tasks. He initiated the project of rebuilding Jerusalem's walls and the broken lives of the people. At the outset of the project we find enemies ridiculing Nehemiah. Sanballat and Tobiah labeled the rebuilding of Jerusalem's walls a "rebellious act." They also said the walls could never be rebuilt because the damage was too extensive (Nehemiah 2:19). Nehemiah 4:1-3 states, *"Sanballat was very angry when he learned that we were rebuilding the wall." "He flew into a rage, and insulted and mocked us and laughed at us, and so did his friends and the Samaritan army officers." "What does this bunch of poor, feeble Jews think they are doing?" he scoffed. "Do they think they can build the wall in a day if they offer enough* sacrifices? *"And look at those charred stones they are pulling out of the rubbish and using again!"* Tobiah, who was standing beside him remarked, *"if even a fox walked along the top of their wall, it would collapse!"(4)* Ridicule can cut deeply, causing discouragement and despair. What did Nehemiah do in the face of this opposition? He **_prayed_** and the work continued. The scoffers continued to oppose Nehemiah and the people in every way imaginable in an attempt to thwart the building project. They were unsuccessful. The wall was completed in fifty-two days! The Bible says in Nehemiah 6:16, *"When our enemies and the surrounding nations heard about it, they were frightened and humiliated, and they realized that the work had been done with the help of our God."(*4)* The unsaved nations ended up giving God the Glory! That's truly amazing!

There are other characters in the Bible who were chosen by God to do incredible things. Remember David, the little Shepherd boy? He's the one who killed the giant Goliath. God chose him over his older brothers to become the second and most favorite King of Israel. King David is the writer of most of the Psalms we all get so much inspiration from. Remember Joseph and how he was despised by his brothers because they were filled with jealousy and envy toward him. They hated him and could not say a kind word to him (Genesis 37:4). One day his brothers threw him in a pit and talked about killing him. They changed their minds about killing Joseph but conspired to sell him to the Ishmeelites instead. Genesis 37:28 reads, *"The Midianites were passing by and it was **they** who lifted up Joseph out of the pit and sold Joseph to the Ishmeelites, for twenty pieces of silver: and they brought Joseph into Egypt."(KJV)* When his brother Reuben returned to the pit, he found it empty. Joseph's brothers then took his coat and dipped it in the blood of a young goat which they had killed. They took the blood soaked coat to their father Jacob and told him Joseph had been killed by an evil beast. The news broke Jacob's heart and the Bible says he mourned for his son for many days. This story shows the great lengths that some will go, once their jealousy and envy has pushed them to the "breaking point." Joseph may have been picked "on" but God picked him "out" to be the "preserver" of their lives, save Egypt, and prepare the way for the beginning of the nation of Israel.

When others intend evil for your life, remember that they are only God's tools. *"Greater is he that is in you, than he that is in the World."* God can transform those who are picked "on" to become those who are picked "out" to bring honor and Glory to his name! Learn how to trust him to do just that....

"Be not dismayed what e'er betide,"
"God will take care of you;"
"Beneath His wings of love abide,"
"God will take care of you."
"God will take care of you,"
"Thru ev'ry day, O'er all the way;"
"He will take care of you,"
"God will take care of you."

*(Hymn by Civilla D. Martin *6)*

Chapter 3

"Anger"

Anger – The feeling one has toward something or someone that hurts, opposes, offends, or annoys; strong displeasure. To irritate or inflame. (*9)

Defuse – To remove the fuse or slow burning wick. The removal of other devices used to set off a shell, bomb, or blast of gunpowder. To make less harmful, potent, or tense: Calm. (*9)

Fact – Sometimes in our dealings with others, we lose patience and say things that we shouldn't say. Once words are released, they can't be taken back.

TRUTH – *"But now put away and rid yourselves (completely) of all these things: anger, rage bad feeling toward others, curses and slander, and foulmouthed abuse and shameful utterances from your lips!" (Colossians 3:8 Amplified Bible)*

TRUTH - *"A soft answer turns away wrath, but grievous words stir up anger." (Proverbs 15:1 Amplified Bible)*

"CHOOSE TO DEFUSE"

If you pay close attention to the daily media reports, you will clearly see that anger, rage, and widespread violence are increasing epidemics sweeping the face of our nation. Our media personnel, in an effort to increase their Nielsen Ratings, take an "if it bleeds it leads" approach to the types of stories that are chosen as their headlines. The constant exposure only fuels the negativity more with many anxiously awaiting their "five minutes of fame." What is the driving force behind all of this? **ANGER**. Look at the word "ANGER" for a moment. If you add a "D" to the beginning of it you get **"DANGER."** "Road Rage," "violence in the workplace," "school shootings," "gang violence," etc, are all the by product of a rage filled society. Some, in an effort to control their anger, have enrolled themselves in Anger Management classes. Conflict, strife, disrespect, and a simple case of "not treating my neighbor as I want to be treated," has led to a rash of violence, the likes of which has never been witnessed before.

The old adage "it takes two to argue" is true. Taking the "high" road by avoiding conflict is not readily accepted by our more modern day society. It is for the sake of "pride" that offenses are not overlooked or quickly forgiven. We can't and often don't allow many offenses to slip pass us without retaliating in some form or another. Most would rather "infuse" than "defuse." By this I mean add fuel to the fiery argument than water. So what's the remedy? *"Choose to Defuse."* Deuteronomy 30:19 states: *"I call heaven and earth to record this day against you that I have set before you life and death, blessing and cursing: therefore choose life, that thou and thy seed may live."(KJV)* There are always two doors in life for us to walk through or two paths for us to walk down, **Right** or **Wrong!** The choice is our own to make. Once the choice is made, we then have to live with the outcome and consequences of our actions. Is "anger" really that dangerous? After all, the Bible does tell us to "Be angry and sin not." This is true; however, **"sin not"** should always be the emphasis. An example of this would be when Jesus was in Jerusalem and he went into the temple with a whip and began to cast out them that sold and bought (Luke 19:45). Jesus displayed a "righteous indignation" over the blatant sins being committed in the house of God. Sin is nothing to play around with and has to be confronted head on and dealt with in a serious manner.

The type of anger I'm alluding to is how we react when someone "pushes our buttons" and we find ourselves "pushed to the limit," "the breaking point," "the point of no return." How should we respond? As I write these words, I'm reminded of a familiar Bible passage found in the 20th chapter of the book of Numbers. Our story unfolds in the wilderness of Zin. Moses is bombarded with the constant murmurings and complaints of the Children of Israel against him and God. After everything God and Moses had done for them, they still found it in their hearts to be unthankful and ungrateful. We as Christians must always display an "attitude" of "gratitude" towards God for his many many blessings bestowed upon us. When we are not thankful, God is not pleased with us. The people gathered themselves against Moses and Aaron and complained that there was no food or water to drink. Moses and Aaron consulted the Lord for the answer to the problem. The Lord tells Moses to take his rod and Aaron, and then gather the people together. Moses was then instructed by God to "speak" unto the **rock (Jesus)** before the people and it would give forth water. Numbers 20:10-12 reads: *"And Moses and Aaron gathered the congregation together before the rock, and he said unto them, hear now ye rebels; must we fetch you water out of this rock? And with his rod he smote the rock twice: and the water came out abundantly, and the congregation drank, and their beasts also. And the Lord spake unto Moses and Aaron, because ye believed me not, to sanctify* *me in the eyes of the Children of Israel, therefore ye shall not bring this congregation into the land which I have given them."(KJV)* It may seem that Moses committed a "small" infraction in light of everything good he had done previously. But in God's eyesight, it wasn't. There were some serious offenses committed by Moses. In verse ten we find him taking credit for himself for what God had done, harshly addressing the people by calling them rebels, and being provoked about their need which resulted in resentment. Moses was the leader and the model for the whole nation. His direct disobedience dishonored God in the presence of his people. Moses' fit of rage cost him and Aaron the opportunity to enter the Promised Land. "The danger of anger."

The Bible's next example is that of a person who "Chose to Defuse" when placed in the position to lash out in anger. It is in I Samuel Chapter 18 that we pick up the story of David. David has just slain the Philistine Giant Goliath and King Saul takes him from his father's house to live in the palace with him. Saul sets David over the men of war. He is accepted in the sight of all the people, and also in the sight of Saul's servants. Everything is fine until the twin demons, "jealousy" and "envy" surface. The women came out of the cities of Israel joyously singing, dancing with tabrets and musical instruments to meet King Saul. The women answered one another as they played and said: *"Saul hath slain his thousands, and David his ten thousands."* The Bible says in verses 8, 9-12: *"And Saul was very wroth and the saying displeased him. And Saul eyed David from that day forward."(KJV)* The text goes on to tell us that the next day when an evil spirit came upon Saul, David played his harp for him as he had done many times before. A jealous filled Saul had a javelin in his hand and cast it at David to kill him. But David escaped out of harm's way twice. From that day forward, Saul was in "hot" pursuit of David to slay him. Saul was jealous of David's popularity. In spite of this, David continued to do right by Saul (Defuse).

16

Saul was intimidated by David's strengths and thus made aware of his own shortcomings and failures. Saul's frustration and anger really wasn't with David, it was with himself. David on the other hand, had great respect for Saul even though he was trying to kill him. Saul may have been in a state of sin and rebellion against God, but David respected the position he held as God's anointed King. David knew that in God's own time, he would be King and "one reaps what he sows." This is an example to us to respect and honor those who have the rule over us no matter how difficult they are to get along with. Psalm 75 tells us *"promotion comes from the Lord...He puts down one and sets up another."(KJV)* God knows what's *best for us* and he knows what it takes to bring the *best out of us*. God uses difficult people to build necessary Christian Character in us so we will be fit for the Master's use. After reading about David's dealings with Saul, I know that I can "Choose to Defuse" as well. I don't have to lash out at others in anger. I'm believing God for growth in this area everyday. I'm sure none of us have someone chasing us trying to kill us as was the case with David. If he was able to "turn the other cheek," so can we. Learn how to overcome evil with good.

"Defusing," contrary to popular opinion, does not make one a coward, wimp, or sissy. It makes you very courageous and wise. Remember, we are not responsible for how others treat us. We are responsible and accountable to God for how we treat them! Jesus, the "Master Diffuser," told us to *"Love your enemies; Bless them that curse you."* Being good to those who mistreat you is not easy but it is necessary if you want to please the Father. Remember Jesus words while he was on the cross dying, *"Father forgive them for they know not what they do."* We too are to take the position of a "Diffuser" and not confuse others by our behavior. If we tell the world that we are a Christian but fail to **_demonstrate_** the principles of the Bible, we lose our witness and effectiveness for God. God knows our behaviors and dispositions don't change overnight, just ask the disciple Peter. Peace, however strong the challenge, must be our ultimate goal. Jesus is our greatest example. With him living on the inside of us enabling us to do so, we too can "Choose to Defuse" in our everyday dealings with difficult people. Apart from Christ, there will be limited success in the "Anger Management" department. The harvest that springs from an anger driven life is one that will be very unpleasant and unrewarding to the sower! "Choose to Defuse." If you don't, God will most assuredly, "refuse" you…

"It is no secret what God can do."
"What he's done for others, he'll do for you."
"With arms wide open, he'll pardon you."
"It is no secret what God can do."

(Hymn by Stuart Hamblen *6)

Chapter 4

"Appointment"

Appointment — A meeting with someone at a certain time and place, engagement. (*9)

Fact — No one likes the thought of dying or losing a precious loved one to death. Death is the one subject that most people do *NOT* like to discuss.

TRUTH — *"And it is appointed unto men once to die, but after this the judgment:" (Hebrews 9:27 KJV)*

"THE REALITY OF DEATH"

Death is the one "appointment" on each of our calendars that we **all** must keep! This appointment will not be cancelled or missed by anyone who has God's breath in his or her lungs. The only logical way someone could miss death is if that person had never been born in the first place! God tells us in his word that everyone has an appointment with death, and after death, the *judgment.* James 4:14 states: *Whereas ye know not what will be on the morrow. For what is your life: it is even a vapour, that appeareth for a little time and then vanisheth away."(KJV)* There is no escape and no getting around it. We all have to leave here. Life as we know it will one day be over. Will you be ready? We are all going to live forever. That's an absolute! The question remains, WHERE? Will we be in Heaven, with the Father, Son, and Holy Ghost? Or will we end up in hell, with the devil and his demons? We are making our choice every day we live as to where our eternal residence will be!

Most people in general do not want to accept the truth that they are going to die one day. Some are afraid of dying and thus believe by ignoring the subject and not talking about it will somehow prevent death from coming their way. Some think they are too young to die. Others believe they are invincible and are silly enough to think they can cheat or outsmart death. The Christian sees death differently. The Apostle Paul stated in Philippians 1:21, *"For to me to live is Christ, and to die is gain."(KJV)* This is our greatest hope! We Christians know this world is not our home. We are foreigners living in a "strange" land. We are "pilgrim travelers." We are just passing through! Christians are ambassadors for Christ here on earth. While here, we will do the Master's will and purpose for our lives that He is calling us to do. We are citizens of Heaven anxiously awaiting our glorious and victorious return trip home! We will finally be free from this mean and sinful world!

Many people by their behavior, ways and actions, make it seem as though they are going to be here forever. Many don't believe the Bible and it's message. They don't believe Jesus is coming back and rapture His church. They view this teaching as something which has been said by "weak" minded people for hundreds of years. It has not nor will it ever come to pass. It is only a fairy tale! Because of this ideology, most go about making their plans for this life only, with no preparation being made for the life that is to come after death. What's a lifetime in comparison to eternity? The main focus of most people consists of: *"their education," "where they work," "how much money they make and have saved or invested," "what type of car they drive," "the house and neighborhood they live in," "their body/how they look," "their image," "prestige," "honor," "their material possessions," "their family," "the vacation trips they take each year,"* and most important of all, *"retirement!"* Simply stated, the "cares of the world," leaving little or no time spent seeking the things of the Lord. God is not in their thoughts until trouble shows up. They are bombarded with **"The Lust of the flesh," "The Lust of the eyes,"** and **"The Pride of life."** These are the very three temptations which caused the fall of "Man" in the Garden of Eden. They want God's blessings from His hands but they don't want to seek His face and surrender their life to Him. They want to use God part-time, but they don't want Him to rule or govern their lives. Jesus states: *"For what is a man profited, if he shall gain the whole world, and lose his own soul?"(Matt 16:26) (KJV).* In Luke 12:16-21, Jesus tells a compelling parable of a rich fool. *"And he spake a parable unto them saying, the ground of a certain rich man brought forth plentifully: And he thought within himself, saying, what shall I do, because I have no room where to bestow my fruits? And he said, this will I do: I will pull down my barns and build greater; and there will I bestow* *all my fruits and my goods. And I will say to my soul, soul, thou hast much goods laid up for many years; take thine ease, eat, drink and be merry. But God said unto him, thou fool this night thy soul shall be required of thee: then whose shall those things be, which thou hast provided? So is he that layeth up treasures for himself, and is not rich toward God"* **(KJV).** This passage of scripture lets us know that planning for retirement is wise but our focus should not be just to enrich ourselves with little or no concern for helping others. Our "earthly" actions carry "heavenly" consequences to be meted out in eternity!

The spiritual condition of our souls is serious business and should not be taken lightly. We only receive one chance in life to get our soul right with God. Most don't see it this way however. Many feel they are morally good and some even claim to live "cleaner" lives than most "so called," "Bible carrying," "scripture quoting Christians." Morally good is not good enough to enter God's kingdom! We can only enter Heaven through and by the blood of our Lord and Savior Jesus Christ. Apart from his atoning grace, we are eternally lost. Satan is very crafty and cunning. He sets traps for people in order to get their soul. He's careful to blind their "minds" so that they are not made aware of the destructive plans he has set for them. Many don't even realize they belong to him since they have never verbally pledged their allegiance to him. The problem is, they haven't given their heart and lives to Jesus either. In cases such as this, the person unknowingly "defaults" to serving and being under the influence of Satan. Being a "bad" person is not what makes one a candidate for hell! The blood of Jesus washes sin away. Rejecting Christ as Lord and Savior is what gains one entry to hell for all eternity. We are currently in the Dispensation of Grace. God is being merciful to mankind and trying to give everyone a chance to become "saved" by accepting his Son Jesus as their personal Savior. God desires that all men come to repentance. He does not want to see anyone perish. There is nothing in this world worth going to hell over but countless people, sad to say, are on that crowded road leading to destruction.

The devil is real and hell is real. The devil, by most, has been relegated to a fairy tale creature having two horns, wearing red pajamas, and holding a pitchfork. The devil is not a fairy tale creature or myth. He is a very real and powerful Archangel. Although powerful, the devil is not omniscient. He is not all knowing. He is not omnipresent, so he can't be everywhere at the same time. Finally, he is not omnipotent, and that means all powerful! These are the true characteristics of God. With the help of his many demons though, the devil has wrecked havoc on the earth since his fall from heaven (Isaiah 14 and Ezekiel 28). Jesus tells us *"The thief cometh not but for to steal, and to kill, and to destroy: I am come that they might have life, and that they might have it more abundantly."(John 10:10 KJV)* Most people don't want the abundant life promised to them by Christ. They want to achieve their abundant life on their own terms and outside of God. Christians follow Matthew 6:33 which states: *"But seek ye first the kingdom of God, and his righteousness; and all these things shall be added unto you."(KJV)* Hell is the place of departed souls and spirits of "man." Hell is not the grave! It is a place of torment located in the heart of the earth originally created by God for the devil and his angels. The unrighteous go to hell at death. There they will remain until the final judgment of the lost (2 Peter 2:9), when all the unsaved and hell itself, will be cast into the lake of fire (Revelation 20:13-15). There are examples in the Bible that show what happens to those who do not have a "reality of death." What we do on this side of "life" will ultimately determine what is done to us on the other side of death.

"Man" is a triune being. "Man" is a spirit, he has a soul, and he lives in a body. Physical death is the separation of the soul and spirit from the body. Spiritual death is the eternal, complete, final separation from God. When a person

23

dies, his body goes back to the dust awaiting the resurrection. The spirit (seat of knowledge) and soul (seat of feeling and appetite) live forever from the body either in Heaven enjoying peace, joy, and love forevermore with the Lord, or in hell, suffering continuous pain and torment at the hands of Satan. The spirit and soul are fully conscious when a person dies. Luke 16:19-31 is concrete evidence of what takes place after death when a righteous and unrighteous person dies.

In this passage, Jesus tells a parable of the Rich Man and Lazarus. The rich man had everything he wanted. In starch comparison, a poor, crippled and diseased beggar (Lazarus) had nothing. In the course of time, both men die. Lazarus goes to Abraham's bosom. This was a place of paradise for all Old Testament believers at the time of death. The rich man is buried and this is what transpired next. Verses 23 -28 read as thus from the Amplified Bible: ***"And in Hades (the realm of the dead), being in torment, he lifted up his eyes and saw Abraham far away, and Lazarus in his bosom. And he cried out and said, Father Abraham, have pity and mercy on me and send Lazarus to dip the tip of his finger in water and cool my tongue, for I am in anguish in this flame. But Abraham said, Child, remember that you in your lifetime fully received comforts and delights, and Lazarus in like manner the discomforts, and distresses, but now is he comforted here and you are in anguish. And besides all this, between us and you a great chasm has been fixed, in order that those who want to pass from this place to you may not be able, and no one may pass from there to us. And the rich man said, then, father, I beseech you to send him to my father's house for I have five brothers, so that he may give solemn testimony and warn them, lest they too come into this place of torment."***

This passage of scripture clearly shows that although the rich man was in torment, he had feelings. He was able to reason thus proving that his soul and spirit were together.

He was fully aware of what was happening to him and there was nothing he could do to stop it. He will experience this torture and anguish for all eternity. Don't let this story be made a reality to you. It is in the Bible for our warning. Commit to memory Hebrews 9:27, *"And it is appointed unto men once to die, but after this the judgment."* We all will live forever! The question is **where** and **with whom?** The decision? We make it **today**. WHY? We know *"The Reality of Death!"*

"O, Lord haste the day when my faith shall be sight,"
"The clouds be rolled back as a scroll;"
"The trump shall resound and the Lord shall descend,"
"Even so it is well with my soul."

(Hymn by Horatio G. Spafford *6)

"O I want to see Him, look upon his face,"
"There to sing forever of his saving grace;"
"On the streets of Glory let me lift my voice;"
"Cares all past, home at last, ever to rejoice."

(Hymn by R. H. Cornelius *6)

Chapter 5

"Arena"

Arena − A Roman amphitheater used for gladiatorial combats; any place of conflict or trial. (*8 & *9)

Fact − Words, whether positive or negative, shape our beliefs about ourselves. Sad to say, we hear more negative words than positive ones. The beliefs formed, will ultimately be played out by the behavior and conduct demonstrated during the course of our lives.

TRUTH − *"For we wrestle not against flesh and blood, but against principalities, against powers, against the rulers of this world, against spiritual wickedness in high places."* *(Ephesians 6:12 KJV)*

TRUTH − *"For the weapons of our warfare are not carnal, but mighty through God to the pulling down of strongholds; casting down imaginations, and every high thing that exalteth itself against the knowledge of God, and bringing into captivity every thought to the obedience of Christ."* *(2nd Corinthians 10:4-5 KJV)*

"THE BATTLE IS ON!"

"You are so ugly!" "You are dumb and won't amount to anything just like your no good father/mother." "You are a loser!" "You don't have good hair like I do." "You are too dark." "You're a brunette, blondes have all the fun." "Four eyes!" "You never went to college?" "You are a failure in life." "You were born out of wedlock?" "Nobody likes you." "You don't have any talent!" "Goody two shoes!" "Nerd!" "Why can't you be more like your brother/sister?" "Boys are better at math/computers than girls." "You were an accident/mistake." "I really wanted to have a boy/girl." "I never loved you." "I want a divorce." "The wedding is off!" "Why are you still single, are you gay?" "Why don't you kill yourself and get it over with." "Christians are weak minded people who use church as their crutch." "My spiritual gift is better and more important than yours." "You committed a sin after your were saved and you still call yourself a Christian?" "There is no way God is ever going to forgive someone like you!" "You are wasting your time reading that Bible and going to church!" "Who wants to be saved, there is no fun in that!" "You know the pastor and deacons are stealing all the money from the church don't you?" "It doesn't take all that to be saved!" "God could never use you for his service." "God never called women to preach/teach the Gospel." "The church is full of nothing but hypocrites!" "Christians are poor, they don't have nothing, that's why I'm not one!" "I have much more than you do and I don't go to church."

Originally created by the Romans, the arena was an amphitheater that was used for the distinct pleasure of gladiatorial combats. The Romans persecuted thousands of Christians for not worshiping official Roman gods.

27

Countless Christians were martyred during this time for their faithful witness and stance for God. Unarmed with conventional weapons, they were put in the arena with ferocious animals or at times an armed warrior. The fight was to the death physically but not spiritually! The Christian's faithfulness to God even on pangs of death, earned them eternal life spent with God! The slaughtering of Christians is still practiced today in certain countries. This level of persecution however has not reached the Christians here in the Western World. Does this mean we are safe? Of course not! 1st Peter 5:8-9 states: ***"Be sober, be vigilant; because your adversary the devil as a roaring lion, walketh about, seeking whom he may devour."(KJV)*** Christians ***PRAY*** and the Devil ***PREYS!*** He uses every means he can to destroy us! His most deadly weapon of choice however is deceptive "mind games." Words and messages play a vital role in the success or failure of the devil in our life. He'll use fear, doubt of God's word, anxiety, insecurity, inferiority complexes, our past, etc., to bring us down. He will succeed if we buy into the lie and deception he's feeding us. This is why our thinking has to be in line with the word of God. Whatever the thoughts are, the actions and conduct will follow suit. Right thinking produces right actions. Wrong thinking produces wrong actions. It's that simple. God's word has the remedy of course. The Apostle Paul sums it up in Philippians 4:8: ***"Finally, brethren, whatsoever things are <u>true</u>, whatsoever things are <u>honest</u>, whatsoever things are <u>just</u>, whatsoever things are <u>lovely</u>, whatsoever things are of <u>good report</u>; if there be any virtue, and if there be any praise, <u>think</u> on these things."(KJV)***

"Words," "words," "words," "voices," "voices," "voices," "messages," "messages," "messages." From our mother's womb, the hearing of "messages" starts. From the day of our birth, the programming of our minds begins. The battle is officially on! My mom once told me that "you can't help the negative things that others say about you, your job is to just make sure that the things they say are not true." This is a pearl of wisdom that I strive to live my life by each and everyday. We must remind ourselves that people don't define who we are, God *does*. The opinion God has about us is the one that truly counts in the end. The music we listen to, the television programs, DVD's and videos we watch, the things we read, our every day conversation, and most importantly, the company we keep, all help to shape our minds in more ways than we know. Words are very powerful and go a long way. Words have lasting emotional affects on us remaining sometimes until we close our eyes in death. Some words are good and come to us when we are down, lifting us up, bringing great cheer. Some words are bad however, and come to us when we are feeling happy and upbeat, leaving us sad, broken, and depressed. The devil is very clever. He often comes to us as a wolf in sheep clothing presenting a false and misleading message. There is a big difference between "constructive" criticism and "destructive" criticism. The aim of "constructive" criticism is to build up character and promote healthy self esteem. It is done in love. "Destructive" criticism's aim is to tear a person down promoting low self esteem. It is done with malice and contempt. An example of constructive criticism would be the account of Priscilla, Aquila, and Apollos over in the 18th chapter of the book of Acts. Apollos was an eloquent man and mighty in the scriptures. He came to Ephesus fervent in the spirit. He spoke and taught diligently the things of the Lord, knowing only the baptism of John. He did not know about the Holy Spirit's baptism. He spoke boldly in the synagogue and Priscilla and Aquila heard him. Rather than correct Apollos publicly, Priscilla and Aquila, in an act of love, invited him to their home and explained to him the way of God more adequately. Because of this, Apollos went on to Achacia where he was mightily used of God for the furtherance of the Gospel. Weigh everything you hear by the Spirit of God and his awesome and powerful Word. You will never go wrong if you do that.

Look at the list of sayings you just read. Were any of them ever said about you or directly to you? Did you believe the statement when it was made to you? How did it affect you? Have you ever reciprocated the same to others? I find myself on both sides of the coin. I've been told quite a few of those things on the list and out of meanness told them to others. Thank God for the atoning grace of Jesus. Any man in Christ is a new creature. During the course of your day, how many positive statements do you hear as opposed to negative ones? Your thoughts and the words you say, are they more about positive righteous things or negative sinful things? The answer to that question will ultimately depend on what "images" and "messages" we allow to take root in our minds and hearts becoming a part of us. What we allow our eyes to see, ears to hear, mouth to say, will most assured become thoughts. Thoughts we must remember will be the bridge to the good or bad behavior we demonstrate. The battle is for the mind. The mind is the "arena," the place of conflict or trial. It is in the mind where our battles with the devil and sin will either be won or lost. Remember, your "attitude" determines your "altitude." If you think *"I can,"* you will! If you think *"I can't,"* you won't! You are your own worse enemy. What you think about the future determines how you live in the present. Remember the story of the "Little Engine That Could." The little engine made it over the mountain because it kept saying over and over as it **_approached_** the mountain, *"I think I can," "I think I can," "I think I can."* In other words, the decision to make it over the mountain was already made! The little engine had a well made up mind to conquer and not avoid the adversity set before it. Jesus tells us in Matthew 9:29: *"According to your faith, be it unto you."*

David is a great example of this. It is in the 17th chapter of I Samuel where we find the giant Goliath defying the camp of Israel. For forty days, morning and evening, he draws near to Israel's camp taunting and challenging them to a fight. Goliath was definitely a "high thing" exalting

30

himself against the knowledge of God that had to come down! David, the little shepherd boy, heard him one day taunting as before, and he has this response in verse 26: *"And David spoke to the men that stood by him saying, what shall be done to the man that killeth this Philistine, and taketh away the reproach from Israel? For who is this uncircumcised Philistine, that he should defy the armies of the living God?"(KJV)* King Saul is told what David said and sends for him. Verses 32 & 33 reads: *"And David said to Saul, let no man's heart fail because of him; thy servant will go and fight this Philistine. And Saul said to David, thou are <u>not able</u> to go against this Philistine to fight with him for <u>thou art but a youth,</u> and he a man of war from his youth."* Does David allow what Saul said to him scare him or change his mind? No! Why not? He was definitely over matched physically. Physically, that's a fact, but not spiritually, and that's the **truth!** Where does David's confidence come from? The answer is found in verses 34 & 35. David gives Saul his testimony. He tells Saul the story about the time when he kept his father's sheep. There came a lion and a bear that took a lamb out of the flock. He rescues the lamb and kills both the lion and the bear. As far as David is concerned, Goliath is just like them, nothing more than a wild animal that will be put to death. It was no doubt in David's mind that he would prove victorious over the Giant. Verse 37 reads: *"David said, moreover, the Lord that delivered me out of the paw of the lion, and out of the paw of the bear, he will deliver me out of the hand of the Philistine."(KJV)* David had already defeated Goliath where? In the arena of his mind! Each victory the Lord helps us win, will give us the faith and courage we need to "press" through and win the next one too! David knew if God did it before, He was well able to do it again! *If God be for us, who can be against us?"*

Saul gave David his war clothes. David tried them on but ultimately told Saul he could not use them because they had not been proven or tested. Besides, David had on the

31

whole armor of God. He did not need any help from "man."
Some may say David talked courageously in Saul's presence
but wonder how he responded once he finally met Goliath
face to face. Verse 45- 46, 50 reads: ***"Then said David to
the Philistine, thou comest to me with a sword, and with a
spear, and with a shield; but I come to thee in the name of
the Lord of hosts, the God of the armies of Israel, whom
thou hast defied. This day will the Lord deliver thee into
my hand, I will smite thee; and give the carcass of the host
of the Philistine this day unto the fowls of the air, and to
the wild beasts of the earth; that all the earth may know
that there is a God in Israel. So David prevailed over the
Philistine with a sling and with a stone and smote the
Philistine, and slew him."(KJV)*** Mighty mighty powerful
words of faith from a youngster! David did not need a
physical sword to kill Goliath because he had a ***spiritual one.***
He used the word of God! Hebrews 4:12 tells us: ***"For the
word of God is quick, and powerful, and sharper than any
two edged sword, piercing even to the dividing asunder of
soul and spirit, and of the joints and marrow, and is a
discerner of the thoughts and intents of the heart."(KJV)***

All of us have "Goliaths" in our lives that need to be
cast down. Remember, we are in a "continuous" spiritual
war with Satan who never gives up in his desire to destroy
us. What high thing are you allowing to exalt itself against
the knowledge of God? What battle is taking place right
now in the "arena" of your mind? What negative words is
the devil and people used of the devil, saying to you? Cast
them down in the name of Jesus! Romans 12:2 reads, ***"And
be not conformed to this world: but be ye transformed by
the renewing of your mind, that ye may prove what is that
good, and acceptable, and perfect, will of God."(KJV)***
Study and apply God's word everyday! Remember to always
pray. If you pray, you'll stay. If you fast, you'll last. If you
don't you won't. Learn to build yourself up in the spiritual
things of the Lord. Remember, this is warfare. And as such
is the case with war, there are many many battles. Don't

think the devil is only going to attack you once and leave you alone. He's like the Energizer Bunny, he keeps coming and coming. Every round goes higher and higher. Be ready and on guard. How can you ensure you will win the battles in the arena of your mind? By committing to memory and practice Joshua 1:8, *"This book of the law shall not depart out of thy mouth; but thou shalt meditate therein day and night, that thou mayest observe to do according to all that is written therein; for then thou shalt make thy way prosperous, and then thou shalt have good success! (KJV)* The word of God will work, if you work the word of God!

"I must tell Jesus all of my trials,"
"I cannot bear these burdens alone;"
"In my distress He kindly will help me,"
"He ever loves and cares for His own."

(Hymn by Elisha A. Hoffman *6)

Chapter 6

"Arrive"

Arrive - To reach an end of a journey; come to a place. To be successful; establish position or reputation. (*9)

Fact - Everyone has character flaws. If we paid more attention to correcting "ourselves" and not others, the world would be a much better place.

TRUTH - *"And why beholdest the mote that is in thy brother's eye, but considerest not the beam that is in thine own eye? Or how wilt thou say to thy brother, let me pull out the mote out of thine eye: and behold, a beam is in thine own eye? Thou hypocrite, first cast out the beam out of thine own eye; and then shalt thou see clearly to cast out the mote out of thy brother's eye."* *(Matthew 7:3-5 KJV)*

TRUTH - *"As it is written, there is none righteous, no not one....For all have sinned, and come short of the glory of God;"* *(Romans 3:10 & 23)*

TRUTH - *"For not the hearers of the law are just before God, but the doers of the law shall be justified."* *(Romans 2:13)*

"We Haven't Arrived Yet"

As defined by law, females reach the age of maturity at eighteen. Males reach the age of maturity at twenty-one. Although considered mature enough to be labeled as an adult, those well past these ages know we have steadily evolved and matured even more over the years. I thank God I don't have the same mind I did when I was eighteen. At the time however, I thought I would never change.

Progression is the natural way of life. It is an on-going process. There is always more to be learned and experienced in this game called "life." There are "higher heights" and "deeper depths" for us to look forward to. Life is full of stages. Each stage brings with it a wealth of knowledge and wisdom to be used to help others along the way. No matter what stage of life we happen to be in at the moment, we should appreciate and value our time there, but at the same time, look forward to moving on to the next stage ready to learn and evolve even more. For example, a baby doesn't want to remain on a bottle, crawling around and babbling words that no one can understand. A baby naturally starts trying to walk, talk, and eat food from adult plates. Gradually and after much determination, they do arrive at their desired place, the *"Terrible Two's."* The role of the parents and those older are to love, support, guide, guard, and "push" the baby on to maturity. There should never be any hindrances of any kind by anyone to the baby's development. Nature must be allowed to take its rightful course.

Just as "natural maturity" is an on-going process, the same holds true for "spiritual maturity." It too is marked by various "stages" all of which are designed to get us to God's desired place for us. We start out as lambs, drinking the "milk" of God's word. With God's love, support, guidance, guarding, *chastisement,* and "push," we move onward and upward in the things of the Lord. Advancement is to be expected. Eventually, we become sheep, able to eat the "meat" of God's word. Just because we may have matured sooner than others and are now able to eat "spiritual meat," doesn't mean we can sit back and become a judgmental hindrance to those who may be pressing their way to spiritual maturity. We should never be "arrogant," displaying a "superior" attitude. Those who conduct themselves in this fashion, have been tricked by Satan into believing that "they have arrived," and therefore have a license to criticize and belittle others. There are no big "I's" and little "U's" with God. No matter how long we've been saved, how much anointing we may have, or how many Bible verses we've committed to memory, we still have to "grow" and "go" further in the Lord. We should never feel as if we're an "authority" on God and His word, and know all we need to know. As long as we have His breath in our lungs, our *"temples"* are still *"under construction."* God is not finished with us yet. All of us have to take a seat on the "potter's wheel" from time to time. We are all "works in progress" not considered by God to be "finished products." There is always more to be learned and experienced with God. As soon as you think you have Him figured out, He does something so wonderfully magnificent that all you can do is just shake your head in disbelief!

As I write these words, I'm reminded of one of the parables Jesus told found in Luke 10:25–37. In the scripture text, we find Jesus being questioned by a lawyer who was a scholar of Old Testament Law. The lawyer's motive was to trick Jesus into making an erroneous statement so he could be brought before the council. The lawyer may have been an expert in the Mosaic Law with a lot of "Bible knowledge" but he lacked one thing, "wisdom." He did not know how to "apply" what he knew to everyday life situations. The Bible reminds us *"wisdom is the principal thing."* The lawyer suffered, like many today, from a severe case of being so "heavenly minded" that he was no "earthly good." In all his intelligence, he couldn't see "the forest for the trees." In the lawyer's attempt to expose sin in Jesus, he ultimately revealed to himself and those present that it was "he" and not Jesus who had not "arrived yet." He knew the Golden Rule but didn't want to live up to it by loving the unlovable. He harbored ill feelings toward Samaritans in his **_heart_**, and Jesus knew it. Jesus tells the parable of "The Good Samaritan" and asks the lawyer, which one of the three men in the story was the neighbor to the injured man. Verse thirty-seven gives us his response. *"And he said, he that showed mercy on him. Then said Jesus unto him, go, and do thou likewise."(KJV)* Notice what the lawyer said. *"He that showed mercy on him."* If he couldn't find it in his heart to simply *"say"* the word Samaritan, how could he be expected to help one if the situation ever presented itself? This lesson allowed Jesus to prove to the self-righteous lawyer that he had not "arrived" and needed to grow, like most of us, in the area of unconditional love. What most fail to realize is we demonstrate just how much love we truly have for God by the way we treat others. *"If a man say, I love God and hate his brother, he is a liar: for he that love not his brother whom he has seen, how can he love God whom he has not seen? And this commandment have we from him, that he who loves God love his brother also."(I John 4:20-21 KJV)* All of us have certain weaknesses which need "pruning" by the Master. We have motes, beams, and logs in our own eyes so we truly can't point an accusing finger at anyone else. We all come short of the Glory of God. The good news is that God is patient with us. He faithfully and lovingly works with us to get us to *"where"* and *"how"* **_HE_** wants us to be. Pastor Forbes reminds us regularly, *"It takes time to be holy."* It behooves us to remember that when dealing with others. *"As we have therefore opportunity, let us do good unto all men, especially unto them who are of the household of faith." (Ephesians 6:10 KJV)*

Remember, just as we progress and evolve "naturally," we also progress and evolve "spiritually." Don't be afraid to learn more about God and His word. Don't be found guilty of being a self-righteous hindrance to others thereby preventing them from progressing in the Lord, and an even bigger hindrance to yourself, by not allowing the Lord to "grow" you even more. The beginning step to accomplishing this is to constantly remind yourself that *"I have not arrived yet!....."*

"It's me, It's me, It's me oh Lord;"
"standing in the need of prayer,"
"It's me, It's me, It's me oh Lord,"
"Standing in the need of prayer,"
"Not my brother,"
"Not my sister,"
"But it's me oh Lord,"
"Standing in the need of prayer,"
"Not my brother,"
"Not my sister,"
"But it's me oh Lord,"
"Standing in the need of prayer."

(Congregational song. Author unknown)

Chapter 7

"Arrogance"

Arrogance – A feeling of superiority manifested in an overbearing manner of presumptuous claims. Too great pride with contempt for others; haughtiness. (*8 & *9)

Ego/Egotism – Conceit. A thinking, talking, or writing too much of oneself. Excessive use of "I," "My,"& "Me." Selfishness. An exaggerated sense of self importance. (*9)

Pride - 1) A reasonable or justifiable self respect; delight. 2) Proud. Having or showing *excessive* self-esteem. Arrogant, haughty, lofty. (*8)

Ambitious – Too greatly aspiring for fame, success, honor, wealth, or other position. Showy, pretentious, making claims to excellence or importance. (*9)

Fact – There is a big difference between *taking* pride in oneself and *having* pride. The world views prideful, rude, arrogant, selfish, and brash behavior as "confidence," "boldness," "intelligence," and "strength."

TRUTH – *"The fear of the Lord is to hate evil: Pride and arrogancy and the evil way, and the froward mouth do I hate." (Proverbs 8:13 KJV)*

TRUTH –*"Pride goes before destruction, and a haughty spirit before a fall."(Proverbs 16:18 KJV)*

TRUTH — *"This know also, that in the last days perilous times shall come. For men shall be lovers of their own selves, covetous, boasters, proud, blasphemers, disobedient to parents, unthankful, unholy, without natural affection, trucebreakers, false accusers, incontinent, fierce despisers of those that are good, traitors, heady, highminded, lovers of pleasures more than lovers of God; (II Timothy 3:1-4 KJV)*

"LET *GO* YOUR *EGO!*"

"Me," "Myself," and "I" can easily be referred to as the "second trinity" of our contemporary culture. How many times a day do we hear at least one of these three small words used? Vanity and selfishness are character traits which are all too familiar and definitely on the "upward" surge in our society.

It is every man for himself in this "dog eat dog" world. Gone are the good ole' days of preferring or giving space to the "other" person. Young men who willingly give their seat to an elderly woman on a crowded bus/subway or men holding the door to allow ladies to go first are courteous acts "rarely" seen anymore. The Golden Rule, what's that? Nowadays, it is all about "keeping up with The Joneses." Some have even gone so far as to "undermine" and "sell out" their own mother, just to get a "leg up in life." The object of this deceitful game is to stay "one up" on the next person. The motto is: *"climb the corporate ladder by stepping on the next person."* This goal is to be accomplished by any means necessary. Cutthroat tactics and backstabbing ways are the norm in this battle to be number one. The "gloves are off" in this "no holds barred" fight for supremacy. Competitive jealousy is ramped and widespread. It is a very effective tool that has been used by Satan to keep life ever so interesting and spicy. Be watchful of those who "pat" your back. Don't be fooled! They may be feeling for a spot to plunge a knife! There is a tremendous lack of genuine love, kindness, honor, respect and loyalty being demonstrated today. The "faithful few" who possess these qualities are "perceived" as being weak and thus are subjected to chronic mocking, jeering, and scorning. God's word tells us plainly *"meek and humble is the way."* The average person nowadays doesn't want to have anything to do with "humility." Most people are "glory" seekers, striving to make a name for themselves. "Overly ambitious" desires cause them to covet the "limelight" and "spotlight." They do everything they can to make sure they are the center of attention. They will do whatever it takes, and hurt whomever they have to hurt to make sure they succeed and make it to the top! Enron and WorldCom are just two of the many examples of what happens when "Corporate Fat-Cats" abuse their own workers. By compromising their integrity, they misused their employees' retirement money for the sake of material possessions. Their concern was not for their workers' welfare. Their ultimate goals were money, power, and immoral pleasure.

What is behind this behavior? The spirit of **pride**. From the Whitehouse, to the church house, and all the other houses in between, excessive self esteem and haughtiness can easily be found. This is nothing new of course. God has experienced this type of behavior before, firsthand! Ezekiel 28:14 -19 gives the account of the origin of Satan. Satan was the model of perfection, full of wisdom, and perfect in beauty. God anointed Satan as a Guardian Cherub. He was in Eden, the garden of God. Every precious stone adorned him. Since he was a Cherub, he was a part of the "inner circle" of angels who had access to God and guarded His holiness. Satan also was given access to God's holy mountain (Heaven). He had access to the "very" presence of God! When God created Satan, he was perfect and blameless until wickedness was found in him and he sinned. His sin was pride. He became prideful over his beauty and splendor. This is what led to his fall and ultimate judgment. He was expelled from the position of God's Anointed Cherub before His throne. God expelled him and one-third of the angels that sided with him from Heaven. Isaiah 14:12– 14, sheds a little more light into Satan's fall. It clearly depicts the motives of his heart. Read carefully and pay close attention to the ambitious and egotistical statements he makes in this passage of scripture: ***"How art***

thou fallen from heaven, o Lucifer, son of the morning!
How art thou cut down to the ground, which didst weaken
the nations! For thou hast said in thine heart, I will
ascend into heaven, I will exalt my throne above the stars
of God: I will sit upon the mount of the congregation, in
the sides of the north: I will be like the most High."(KJV)
Presently, he walks about as a roaring lion seeking whom he
may devour (I Peter 5:8). His ultimate and final destination
however will be the lake of fire (Revelation 21:10).

Satan's relationship with God is severed forever. He'll
never be able to return back to Heaven. Because of this, his
main objective and desire is to trap and destroy God's most
prized creation, "man." What better way to get back at God.
Satan desires for "man" to suffer the same end time fate as
he and the fallen angels, which is the lake of fire. The sin of
pride has proved to be one of Satan's most effective weapons
of choice to cause "man" to fall. The Bible has many
examples of what happens to those who fall victim to the
deceit of pride. Daniel 4:29-33, gives the account of King
Nebuchadnezzar who had to learn the hard way to *"let go his*
ego," and give praise and honor to the Most High God! His
story is one of the greatest examples of what happens to
those who concentrate too much on "me," "myself," and "I."
Glory, praise, and honor belong to God and God only!
Verses 29-33 reads as thus: *"At the end of twelve months*
He (Nebuchadnezzar) walked in the palace of the kingdom
of Babylon. The king spake and said, is not this great
Babylon, that I have built, for the house of the kingdom by
the might of my power, and for the honor of my majesty.
While the word was in the king's mouth, there fell a voice
from heaven, saying, O King Nebuchadnezzar, to thee it is
spoken; the kingdom is divided from thee. And they shall
drive thee from men, and thy dwelling shall be with the
beasts of the field: they shall make thee eat grass as oxen,
and seven times (years) shall pass over thee, until thou
know that the most High ruleth in the kingdom of men, and
giveth it to whomsoever he will. The same hour was the

43

thing fulfilled upon Nebuchadnezzar: and he was driven from men, and did eat grass as oxen, and his body was wet with the dew of heaven, til his hairs were grown like eagles' feathers and his nails like birds' claws."(KJV) This Bible story is a vivid account of **"pride going before destruction, and a haughty spirit before a fall."** God tells us in His word that He will not share His glory with another. Nebuchadnezzar had to find this out the hard way. God put him on all fours to live as a beast until his pride was no more! In verses 34 & 37, he finally comes to his senses. It reads as thus: *"And at the end of the days I Nebuchadnezzar lifted up mine eyes to heaven, and mine understanding returned unto me, and I blessed the Most High, and I praised and honored him that liveth forever, whose dominion is an everlasting dominion, and his kingdom is from generation to generation: Now I Nebuchadnezzar praise and extol and honor the King of heaven, all whose works are <u>truth</u>, and his ways judgment: and those who walk in pride he is able to abase."(KJV)* God restored Nebuchadnezzar back to his position once he acknowledged Him as King of Kings and Lord of Lords!

Is the spirit of "pride" alive and well only in the "worldly" system which is ruled and governed by Satan? Of course not. Sad to say, this insidious spirit is very much alive in the house of God. In most churches today, the focus of the membership has shifted from "service" to "status." It's not "what" a person knows but "who" he knows that counts. "Church Politics" has replaced the will and desires God He has for His own house. For the right "price," positions are bought and used for selfish gain and not to edify and uplift the name of the Lord. Many are caught up in a "spiritual rat race." Where they are running to only they know. Don't get in their way for you will surely be run over! This is nothing new of course. The Bible has examples of ambitious people who tried to take control of certain positions. Remember the account of the disciples James and John found in Mark chapter 10. Their mother came with them to Jesus and bowed before Him. Her request was that her two sons might be given places of favor in His kingdom. She wanted one son to be seated at Jesus' right hand, and the other son at His left. Jesus asked James and John if they could drink the cup that He was about to drink. Jesus was speaking of His impending trials, betrayal, and death on a cross. They both replied "we can." Jesus indicated they indeed would both share the "cup" of His suffering and death with Him. James suffered death at the hands of Herod Agrippa and John is thought to have died a martyr's death near the end of the first century. When the other disciples heard about the request by James and John's mother, they became angry. Jesus called the twelve together and reminded them of some important principles. Greatness in the Lord's kingdom does not come through rulership or authority but through service. ***"Not by might, nor by power, but by my spirit saith the Lord of hosts."(Zechariah 4:6)(KJV)*** The Apostle John addressed the issue of "domineering ambition" in his Third Epistle addressed to his friend Gauis. In the Epistle, John rebukes Diotrephes who had usurped leadership in one of the churches. He was motivated by love for preeminence in the church. As a result of his personal ambitions, Diotrephes maliciously and slanderously rejected John's authority. He attempted to tear down the reputation of John's representatives. He then refused to "receive the brethren" (traveling ministers to the local church) and put those out of the church that did receive them. He did all he could to force his will on others. Diotrephes was not allowed to continue this type of behavior. When the apostle John arrived, Dotrephes was dealt with accordingly. He too had to learn the hard way to ***"let go his ego."*** The behavior and conduct of Satan, Nebuchadnezzar, James & John, and Diotrephes, should never be copied or imitated. Although the "world" holds prideful and arrogant people in "high" regard, God doesn't. By the "world's" standard, they are considered as "role models," with very "bright futures." God sees them a little differently however. According to his standards, they are "sinful people" with very "dark futures!" Pay close attention to your words. If you find yourself saying *"me," "myself," and "I"* on a regular basis, you are a potential victim of the Sin of "Pride." Don't get ahead of God and try to do your own thing. Better to be "God directed" "than self-driven." The latter will always bring one grief! Remember, *"Pride goeth before destruction, and a haughty spirit before a fall."* Don't let this happen to you! *"Let go your ego!"*

"Praise God from whom all blessings flow,"
"Praise Him all creatures here below."
"Praise Him above ye heavenly host,"
"Praise Father, Son and Holy Ghost."

(Hymn by Thomas Ken *6)

Chapter 8

"Bad Company"

Bad – Evil; wicked, causing harm, unfavorable, rotten, spoiled, offensive, troublesome, not friendly, cross, troublesome, worthless. (*9)

Company – Companion or companions, a gathering of people for social purposes. (*9)

Acquaintance – A person known to one, but **_not_** a close friend. (*9)

Friend – A person who favors and supports. Supporter, patron, helper, advocate. (*9)

Fact – You are known by the company you keep. "True friends will "make" you. So-called friends will "break" you!

TRUTH – *"Can two walk together, except they be agreed?" (Amos 3:3 KJV)*

TRUTH – *"Do not be so deceived and misled! Evil companionships or associations corrupt and deprave good manners, morals, and character." (1ˢᵗ Corinthians 15:33 Amplified Bible)*

TRUTH – *"Be ye not unequally yoked together with unbelievers: for what fellowship hath righteousness with* *unrighteousness? and what communion hath light with darkness?"* *(2ⁿᵈ Corinthians 6:14)*

TRUTH – *"There are "friends" who pretend to be friends, but there is a friend who sticks closer than a brother." (Proverbs 18:24 Life Application Bible)*

"CHOOSE YOUR FRIENDS WISELY!"

There is a verse in an old gospel song I know which says, ***"Bad company will make a good child go astray!"*** Well put! Do you remember hearing this one? ***"If you lay down with dogs, you'll get up with fleas."*** What about this one? ***"Birds of a feather flock together."*** Would you say these old adages are true? I would. They have been proven countless times. Our correctional facilities are over-populated with those who got mixed up with the wrong crowd. They bought into Satan's lies that *"the in crowd is the only crowd to be in"*. *"The cool, hip, fun, brave, strong, people in the know, aren't afraid to live life on the edge!"* *"The square, corny, boring, dull, fearful, weak, old fashioned people worry about being cautious and following the rules."* *"After all, life is short, so play hard!"* *"Don't allow grass to grow under your feet!"* *"You're young!"* *"Be adventurous!"* Many inmates will tell you their parents tried to tell them to do the right thing and stay out of trouble. They on the other hand gave into "peer pressure" and now must deal with the consequences of their actions. Remember, sin will take you farther than you ever planned to go, keep you longer than you ever planned to stay, and cost you more than you ever planned to pay.

The "downward" road is crowded with unsaved people. What many fail to realize however is they are on the "fast track," to nowhere good. Nothing will bring you down faster than the company you keep! You won't be able to soar with *"eagles"* if you find yourself hanging around *"buzzards."* Bad company corrupts good character. Your reputation is what others "say" you are. Your character or conduct is who you "really" are. If you don't like the person you are, you

49

may want to change your company. There is a big difference between "friends" and "acquaintances." We in general are too trusting of others and are quick to label them as "friends" too soon after meeting them. Many are given the title of "friend" and are not worthy of it. You may be a friend to them, but they don't consider themselves a friend to you. The sad thing is, they don't tell you so. You don't find out their true feelings and intent for you until it is too late. My mother always told me **"everyone is not your friend." "You will always be able to count your true friends on one hand and still have fingers to spare."** She was absolutely correct. I had to learn the hard way that some I had been calling "friends" were not really friends at all. They were merely acquaintances. They were "wolves in sheep clothing," on assignment from Satan, sent to destroy me. Dr. Creflo Dollar once said everyone should view their friendships in the same fashion as the set up of the Temple in the Bible. The Temple had three main parts: **The Courts, The Holy Place (where only the priests could enter), and the Holy of Holies (where only the High Priest could enter, and then only once a year, to atone for the sins of the nation-Leviticus 16:1-35)**. This is a very good model for us to use when forming relationships with others. Most relationships, we will find, are **"court"** or **"acquaintance"** relationships. Be careful to watch what you discuss with individuals in this area. Don't trust them with *"sensitive and personal"* information about yourself. Nine times out of ten, you will hear it again from someone else! Remember, acquaintances *are not close friends.* They are merely people that you happen to know. Next we have the **"Holy Place"** relationships. Individuals in this area have more access to you and are therefore closer to you emotionally than those in the "court." They have been given the title of "friend" but only after much time and careful consideration is spent. Lastly, we come to the **"Holy of Holies."** This is the closest "human" access to you which is granted to someone else. It is the most intimate and sacred of all earthly relationships. Only the relationship to God is closer than this one! Due to the serious nature of the "strong emotional bond" and absolute trust needed for "sensitive confidences" shared, the **"Holy of Holies"** relationship should be strictly reserved for a **"best friend" and/ or "spouse."** If you have three people in your "Holy of Holies," I can tell you right now, you have two people too many. Don't give the enemy a crack, for he will come in!

True friendship is earned. It develops over time. It's foundations are: love, trust, respect, sacrifice, honesty, and loyalty. Jealousy and envy are out of the question. Take it from me, a person will never be a "true friend" *to you* while harboring jealousy and envy in their heart *against you!* The twin demons jealousy and envy will always lead to a spirit of "competitiveness." This means they will always try to *"outdo"* or *"outshine"* you. This type of relationship never lasts. If a person can only be your friend as long as you are worse off than they are or beneath them in some fashion, then they are not the person you need to make your allegiance to. A "true friend" will genuinely be glad and support you in your successes as well as be there to help lift you in your times of disappointments. True friends do not enjoy seeing you struggle and have misfortune in your life. Most times without even asking them to, they will be there to help lighten the load and lend a helping hand wherever needed. True friends are able to point out your talents and strengths without harping on your weaknesses and shortcomings. They encourage and motivate you to achieve higher goals instead of enjoying seeing you remain at the same level in life. True friends are not in the relationship only to try and see how much they can get from the relationship. They want to be a contributor as well. As you can see, there aren't too many people who come close to demonstrating this type of behavior. The Bible however has several wonderful examples of what can happen to us and through us when **"we choose our friends wisely!"**

Ist Samuel 18: 1, 3 & 4 gives us a beautiful illustration of the "godly friendship" between David and Saul's son Jonathan. The passage reads as follows, *"And it came to pass, when he (David) had made an end of speaking unto Saul, that the soul of Jonathan was knit with the soul of David, and Jonathan loved him as his own soul. Then Jonathan stripped himself of the robe that was upon him, and gave it to David, and his garments, even to his sword, and to his bow, and to his girdle."(KJV)* David and Jonathan's friendship is one of the deepest and closest recorded in the Bible. It was so because their friendship had a solid foundation, **GOD!** They were first and foremost committed to God, then to each other. They did not allow anything to come between them, not even King Saul, Jonathan's father. They grew closer together when their friendship was tested. They were able to remain friends under all adversity to the end! Although Jonathan realizes that David and not he would be king, he does not allow jealousy and envy to destroy the friendship he and David have. The mark of a godly friendship is when a person can recognize the anointing and gifting in their friend's life without coveting it. They instead will help you arrive at the place where the Lord is taking you! There aren't many who can pass this test right?

Just how close were David and Jonathan? David makes a special tribute to his dearest friend, who along with his father Saul, is killed in battle. 2nd Samuel 1:25 & 26 reads as thus: *"How are the mighty fallen in the midst of the battle! O Jonathan, thou wast slain in thine high places. I am distressed for thee, my brother Jonathan: very pleasant hast thou been unto me: thy love to me was wonderful, passing the love of women."(KJV)* Let me set the record straight! For those who try to use this verse to support homosexual relationships, David was not implying that he and Jonathan had a "sexual" relationship. Leviticus 18:22 and 20:13 shed more light into the sin of homosexuality and the harsh penalty levied to those who practice it. God's ideal for marriage is found in Genesis Chapter 2. David's tribute was simply restating the deep brotherhood and faithful friendship he had with Jonathan and nothing more. There are other "godly" friendships that I'm reminded of in the Bible. In the New Testament, the Apostle Paul had Timothy, Barnabas, Aquila & Priscilla. Jesus had the inner circle disciples Peter, James and John. He also had a close relationship with Mary, Martha and Lazarus. If the Lord and Savior Jesus Christ thought it important to surround himself with "godly" and "true friends," shouldn't we do the same? After all, as the old saying goes, "I can do bad all by myself!" A good example of someone who "did not choose his friends wisely" would be King Rehoboam. His story is found in 2nd Chronicles 10. After Solomon's death, his son Rehoboam is next in line to be crowned king. All of Israel gathers and come to Rehoboam saying: *"Thy father made our yoke grievous: now therefore ease thou somewhat the grievous servitude of thy father, and his heavy yoke that he put upon us, and we will serve thee."* Rehoboam instructs the people to come to him again in three days. He then took counsel with the old men that had stood before Solomon his father. He asks them how he should answer the people. They instruct him that if he is kind to the people, pleases them, and speak good words to them, they will be his servants forever. Rehoboam forsakes the counsel of the old men and takes counsel with the young men that he grew up with. On the third day when the people return to Rehoboam, this is his response to them: *"And the king answered them roughly; and king Rehoboam forsook the counsel of the old men, and answered them after the advice of the young men saying, my father made your yoke heavy, but I will add thereto: my father chastised you with whips, but I will chastise you with scorpions."(2 Chronicles 10:13&14 KJV).* When the people realize what the king is saying, they turn their backs and desert him. Because of Rehoboam's harsh treatment, the nation of Israel splits apart. He tries to unite it with force and is unsuccessful.

He marries heathen women like his father Solomon and ultimately abandons the worship of God by allowing idolatry to flourish. The result was destruction. Listening to the wrong advice cost Rehoboam greatly!

Another example of what happens when one entertains **"bad company"** is found in 2nd Kings Chapter 2. In this chapter, the Lord takes the Prophet Elijah into heaven by a whirlwind. Elisha, his successor, witnesses him being taken up. He then picks up Elijah's mantle and strikes the water of the Jordan with it. This was a plea to God to confirm his appointment as Elijah's successor. Miraculously the water divided and the riverbed dried up so that Elisha, and a companion with him, could cross over. This was the same way the Israelites had crossed the Red Sea and the Jordan River years earlier (*2). With the appointment comes the granting of Elisha's request to have a "double" portion of the prophetic power that Elijah had. Picking it up at verses **23 & 24**: *"And he (Elisha) went up from thence unto Bethel: and he was going up by the way, there came forth little children out of the city, and mocked him, and said unto him, go up, thou bald head; go up; thou bald head. And he turned back, and looked on them, and cursed them in the name of the Lord. And there came forth two she bears out of the wood, and tare forty and two children of them. And he went thence to Mount Carmel, and from there he returned to Samaria."(KJV)* Although the King James Version calls them "little children," it was actually several dozen young men, not children, who confronted Elisha (*2). God's punishment on them was a severe one. By ridiculing the man of God, they were guilty of blaspheming the God he represented (*7). When the God of the Bible says, *"touch not mine anointed and do my servants no harm,"* he means just that. These youths had to find this out the hard way! Whether young or old, being in company with the wrong crowd will prove to be very very dangerous.

The story of Job is a most poignant one when addressing the subject of "choosing friends wisely." As I mentioned earlier, one of the marks of a true friend will be determined when trouble arises. Job's story clearly depicts that those who he thought were good friends, truly weren't there for him when he needed them the most. It is when Job is faced with the greatest sufferings, challenges, and personal traumas of his life that the true character and conduct of those closest to him surface. Satan is permitted by God to attack a "righteous" and "upright" Job. When he is stripped of his children, his wealth, and his health, the first person to hurt him more is his wife. Job 2:9 states: *"Then said his wife unto him, dost thou still retain thine integrity? Curse God, and die."(KJV)* One's mate is the closest and dearest person to them. I can't even begin to imagine the enormous grief Job must have felt at this time. The "turning of backs" by others during difficult times is a hard pill for any of us to swallow. When your mate does it to you however, it cuts even deeper and stings even more! As if his wife wasn't bad enough, Job is then visited by his three friends: **Eliphaz, Bildad, and Zophar.** They come to console Job and to comfort him. Instead of being comforted by them, Job is condemned by them. They do a poor job of comforting Job because they are proud of their own advice and insensitive to Job's needs (*4). They were all under the erroneous assumption that Job was suffering because he had knowingly committed sin and would not admit to God that he had. They believed that good things happen to good people and bad things happen to bad people. Since these bad things have happened to Job then it stands to reason that he must be bad. Their beliefs stemmed from their own experiences and were not true in Job's case. The arrogance and insensitivity of Job's three friends only made him feel worse. In one passage, Job himself says to them: *"miserable comforters are ye all." (Job 16:1 KJV)*

In some instances, Job's friends did show partial knowledge of God's truth and character by some of the statements they made. Their trouble arose when they could not accurately apply the truth to life. They were quick to judge Job without truly knowing what God was doing. Isaiah 55:8 reads as thus: *"For my thoughts are not your thoughts, neither are your ways my ways, saith the Lord."* Our finite minds will never begin to figure out the infinite wisdom of the Almighty! For falsely assuming that Job was guilty and adding to his suffering, Job's three friends are rebuked by God. Job 42:7-8 shows God's anger with them: *"After the Lord had finished speaking with Job, he said to Eliphaz the Temanite: I am angry with you and with your two friends, for you have not been right in what you said about me, as my servant Job was. Now take seven young bulls and seven rams and go to my servant Job and offer a burnt offering for yourselves; and my servant Job will pray for you, and I will accept his prayer on your behalf, and won't destroy you as I should because of your sin, your failure to speak rightly concerning my servant Job"(*4).* Job's three friends were obedient and did what the Lord requested. Job was obedient and also did what the Lord asked. After receiving much criticism *from them*, he was still able to do right *by them.* He prayed for them. Many of us know it's not easy praying for those who have wronged us. Doing it, will definitely test and stretch your faith! It may not be easy but it is necessary if we want to see God. Job, after all he had been through, proved to be a better friend to them than they were to him. This was further validation of his righteousness in the eyes of God. What happened to Job for his obedience in praying for those who had mistreated him? Job 42:10 states: *"Then, when Job prayed for his friends, the Lord restored his wealth and happiness! In fact, the Lord gave him twice as much as before! (*4)*

This proves just how much God loves us. He is a just and fair God who will not only restore whatever we have lost unjustly, but he is *"able to do exceeding abundantly above all that we ask or think!"* Remember, **"choose your** friends wisely." "Bad company" can and will bring you down. You will never "soar with eagles if you hang around buzzards....

> *"What a friend we have in Jesus,"*
> *"All our sins and griefs to bear!"*
> *"What a privilege to carry"*
> *"Everything to God in prayer!"*
> *"O what peace we often forfeit,"*
> *"O what needless pain we bear,"*
> *"All because we do not carry"*
> *"Everything to God in prayer!"*
>
> *(Hymn by Joseph Scriven *6)*

Chapter 9

"Beacon"

Beacon – A light or fire used as a signal to guide or warn. Anything or person that is a guiding or warning signal. (*9)

Wattage – The amount of electric power measured in watts; the power in watts necessary for the operation of an electrical appliance, motor, or the like. (*9)

Incandescent Lamp – A lamp containing a material that gives light by incandescence, especially an electric lamp with a filament of very fine wire that becomes white hot and gives off light when current flows through it. (*9)

Fact – There are many types of religions in the world. Most people believe *all* religions are basically the same. There isn't just one way or path to God, but many.

TRUTH – *"Jesus saith unto him, I am the <u>way</u>, the truth, and the life; no man cometh unto the father, but by me." (John 14:6 KJV)*

TRUTH – *"That at the name of Jesus every knee should bow, of things in heaven, and things in earth, and things under the earth; And that every tongue should confess that Jesus Christ is Lord, to the glory of God the Father." (Philippians 2:10 & 11 KJV)*

"LET YOUR LIGHT SHINE,
NO MATTER THE WATTAGE!"

Have you ever taken a moment and thought about all the wonderful and diverse types of lights there are in the world? The main two of course, are sunlight, and moonlight. But in addition to these are, traffic lights, house lights, light houses, pen lights, flash lights, flood lights, and so on, just to name a few. The most important aspect of these lights is their wattage. The common household light bulb comes in 25, 40 75, and 100 watts. All light bulbs may not have the same wattage, but each is equally important and proves to be significantly valuable when a particular circumstance arises.

For example, a penlight is very handy for us ladies when we lose our keys in our pocket book and are stuck outside our home trying to get in. What happens when a fuse blows? It's the flashlight to the rescue! It provides you with just enough light to get you to the power box to change the fuse. How about that midnight snack? The refrigerator light illuminates the path to that last piece of sweet potato pie! So as you can see, all lights are important and shape our lives in so many different ways. The wattages of the lights may differ, but not the significance! Light removes darkness allowing "man" to see and live. Light is extremely important. Let's look at the sun for a minute. All life on earth, human beings, animals, and plants depend on the heat, light, and other kinds of energy given off by the sun. Without the heat and light of the sun, there could not be any life on the earth (*10). Genesis 1:15 –16 states: *"And God made two great lights; the greater light to rule the day, and the lesser light to rule the night."(KJV)* Just like there cannot be "natural" life without light, there can't be "spiritual" life without light either! St. John 8:12 reads as thus: ***"Then spake Jesus again unto them, saying, I am the light of the world: he that followeth me shall not walk in darkness, but shall have the light of life."(KJV)*** In Christ's light, we see ourselves as we really are (sinners in need of a savior). When we follow Jesus, the Light, we can avoid walking blind and falling into sin. He lights the path for us so that we can see how to live. He removes the darkness of sin from our lives. Death brings eternal darkness, and only Christ's eternal life planted in us will keep us alive in His new kingdom for eternity (*4).

When we Christians live for Christ, we glow like lights, showing others what Christ is like. He has chosen to reflect His light from His followers to an unbelieving world. We have an awesome responsibility to those who are not in the family of Christ. ***"You are the world's light – a city on a hill, glowing in the night for all to see. Don't hide your light! Let it shine for all; let your good deeds glow for all to see, so they will praise your heavenly father." (Matthew 5:14-16 Living Bible)*** All Christians can be viewed as "lamps" fueled and powered by the Holy Spirit. Power from the Holy Spirit involves courage, boldness, confidence, insight, ability, and authority. Don't ever think that your "light" is small, insignificant, and could never be used to bring someone out of darkness into the marvelous light of Christ's love. A little light is better than no light at all! Remember the pen light and refrigerator light? Not much wattage this is true, but proven to be very effective when needed. Never compare what you have and are capable of doing with someone else. Don't try to imitate others. Don't be intimidated, ashamed, or too shy to let your light shine. By the same token, don't be pressured into pretending that your light is "bigger" or more powerful than it really is. Don't fall prey to the senseless game of competitive jealousy. These are just tricks of the enemy to keep you from reaching your full potential in God. Falling victim to these tricks will most assuredly lead to *"power failure!"* Be satisfied with who God has made you to be! Be content with the "wattage" he has given you. You were born with a purpose. You can be a beacon of light that brightens the corner where you are. You can and you will make a difference if you try. God never puts more on us than we can bear. After all, He knows what He's put *in us,* so it stands to reason that He also knows what to expect *from us!* We are not responsible for the measure of faith we have been given. That's the Lord's business. We are however, responsible for utilizing that which has been given to us by the Father. If we prove to be good stewards, the Lord will honor our faithfulness by blessing us with more. The parable about the talents bears this out (Matthew 25: 14-30). Since we are children of light in the Lord, let us walk as children of light. Remember, **"Let your light shine, no matter the wattage!"** Someone somewhere needs what you have. They need to know Christ as their Lord and personal Savior. Let your light be the one that guides them from a stormy raging sea, to the blissfulness of God's celestial shore.

"Trying to walk in the steps of the Savior,"
"Trying to follow our Savior and King,"
"Shaping our lives by His blessed example,"
"Happy, how happy, the songs that we bring."
"How beautiful to walk in the steps of the Savior,"
"Stepping in the light, stepping in the light;"
"How beautiful to walk in the steps of the Savior,"
"Led in paths of light."

(Hymn by Eliza E. Hewitt *6)

Chapter 10

"Blaming Others"

Blame – To hold a person or thing responsible for something bad or wrong. To accuse, find fault with. (*9)

Fact – Blaming others is not hard to do. Taking ownership of one's mistakes is!

TRUTH – *"If we confess our sins, he is faithful and just to forgive us our sins, and to cleanse us from all unrighteousness." (I John 1:9 KJV)*

"DON'T PLAY
THE BLAME GAME"

What does it mean to play the **"Blame Game?"** It simply means to **"pass the buck,"** or make someone/something else the **"scapegoat"** for actions taken and things done. We've all done it at least once in our lifetime. Think back to your childhood days. I'm sure this game was played if for nothing more than to avoid receiving a few "licks" from our parents with a belt or a switch for doing something wrong. No one likes punishment or correction right?

Is the **"Blame Game"** only committed by children or are we adults found guilty of playing it ourselves? Are we sometimes the victims of "Adult Peer Pressure?" I think you know the answer to that one! Here is a list of some of the excuses for improper behavior or conduct that I've heard. Let's see if you've heard any of them. *"I got up on the wrong side of the bed this morning." "I haven't had my first cup of coffee yet." "You know I'm not a morning person." "It's that time of the month." "I'm just a product of my environment." "I was only following orders." "I guess I'm just like my father/mother." "I'm just a sinner saved by grace." "God is not finished with me yet."* And last but surely not least, *"The Devil made me do it."* How many did you recognize? Have you used any of them before? God knows. Is this type of behavior anything new to God? If you look to the Bible you will quickly see that the **"Blame Game"** has been around since the beginning. When King Solomon wrote the words, *"There is no new thing under the sun" (Ecclesiastes 1:9b),* he was absolutely correct. The **"Blame Game"** can be traced back to the very first book of the Bible.

It is in the first few chapters of Genesis that we find the fall of "Man." Adam and Eve break God's commandment by eating from the tree of knowledge of good and evil (Genesis 2:16-17). With the breaking of the commandment comes the **"blame game"** found in Genesis 3:12-13. Adam blames God and Eve, Eve blames the serpent, and the serpent didn't have a "leg to stand on." Did God accept their futile attempts to play the "blame game?" No. This moment of rebellion shattered the perfect creation of God. "Man" now became separated from God and every human being born after would inherit the sinful nature of Adam and Eve. Another example of a person attempting to play the "blame game" is King Saul. In I Samuel chapter 15 we find where the prophet Samuel tells Saul that the Lord is commanding him to **utterly** destroy Amalek. Saul is commanded to destroy everyone and everything from the youngest to the oldest, ox, sheep, camel and ass. Verse 9 states, *"But Saul and the people spared Agag, and the best of the sheep, and the oxen, and of the fatlings, and the lambs, and all that was good, and would not utterly destroy them: but everything that was vile and refuse, that they destroyed utterly."(KJV)* **Partial** or **delayed** obedience is the same as **DISOBEDIENCE.** When Samuel questions Saul about the animal noises he hears in the background, Saul tells him in verse 15, *"They have brought them from the Amalekites: for the people spared the best of the sheep and of the oxen, to sacrifice unto the Lord thy God: and the rest we have utterly destroyed."(KJV)* Saul makes this same statement again in verse 22. He attempts to blame the people for his transgression of the Lord's commandment. Did God accept his excuses? No. In verse 23 Samuel tells Saul, *"Because thou hast rejected the word of the Lord, he hath also rejected thee from being King."(KJV)* In verse 24 Saul in an attempt to save his kingship finally tells Samuel the truth, *"I have sinned: for I have transgressed the commandment of the Lord, and thy words: because I feared the people and obeyed their voice."(KJV)* Saul gave in to "adult peer pressure." Because of this, he loses his throne, the Spirit of the Lord, and ultimately his life.

These two examples show us that there are three enemies to "Man." They are: **The Flesh, The World System, and The Devil.** The word **FLESH** spelled backwards and omitting the "H" is **SELF.** All of us know what a mess **"SELF"** can be don't we? Jesus tells us to *"Deny yourself and take up your cross and follow me."* Paul tells us that in our *"Flesh dwelleth no good thing."(Romans 7:18)* He also tells us in Romans 8:13, *"If ye live after the flesh, ye shall die: but if ye through the spirit do mortify the deeds of the flesh, ye shall live."(KJV)* The second enemy is the **WORLD.** I John 2:15-16 states *"Love not the world, neither the things that are in the world." "If any man love the world, the love of the father is not in him." "For all that is in the world, the lust of the flesh, and the lust of the eyes, and the pride of life, is not of the father, but is of the world."(KJV)* The last enemy to "Man" is the **Devil.** He is referred to as the "Accuser" of The Brethren and "The Tempter." He will do all he can to get you to commit sin.

Although each of us are faced with these three enemies we can't play the "blame game" when we fall short. James 1:14-15 states, *"But every man is tempted when he is drawn away of his own lust, and enticed." "Then when lust is conceived, it bringeth forth sin: and sin when it is finished, bringeth forth death."* In **Deuteronomy 30:19b** God tells us, *"I have set before you life and death, blessing and cursing: therefore choose life, that thou and thy seed may live."(KJV)* Don't play the "blame game." If you make the wrong choice, take ownership of your sin. Repent, confess, and ask God to forgive you. He will. If you don't, he won't.

"Yield not to temptation,"
"For yielding is sin;"
"Each vict'ry will help you"
"Some other to win;"
"Fight manfully onward,"
"Dark passions subdue;"
"Look ever to Jesus,"
"He'll carry you through."
"Ask the Savior to help you,"
"Comfort, strengthen and keep you;"
"He is willing to aid you,"
"He will carry you through."

*(Hymn by Horatio R. Palmer *6)*

Chapter 11

"Bondage"

Bondage – Lack of freedom; slavery. The condition of being under some power or influence. (*9)

Captivity – The condition of being in prison. The condition of being held against one's will. (*9)

Slave – A person who is the property of another. A person who is controlled or ruled by some device, habit or influence. (*9)

Fact – Many people continue in sinful and harmful activities for various reasons. Some find what they are doing pleasurable. Others however, feel that they are "stuck" in their situation and can't get out. They want deliverance from what has them bound but don't know how to go about obtaining it.

TRUTH – *"Jesus replied, you are slaves of sin, every one of you. And slaves don't have rights, but the Son has every right there is! So if the Son sets you free, you will indeed be free." (John 8:34 -36 Living Bible)*

TRUTH – *"The Spirit of the Lord is upon me, because he hath anointed me to preach the gospel to the poor; he hath sent me to heal the brokenhearted, to preach deliverance to the captives, and the recovering of sight to the blind, to set at liberty them that are bruised." (Luke 4:18 KJV)*

TRUTH – *"And you hath he quickened, who were dead in trespasses and sins; wherein times past ye walked according to the course of this world, according to the prince of the power of the air, the spirit that now worketh in the children of disobedience: among whom also we <u>all</u> had our conversation in time past in the lusts of our flesh, fulfilling the desire of the flesh and of the mind; and were by nature the children of wrath, even as others. But God, who is rich in mercy, for his great love wherewith he loved us, even when we were dead in sins, hath quickened us together with Christ, (by grace are you saved;) and hath raised us up together, and made us sit together in heavenly places in Christ Jesus" (Ephesians 2:1 -6 KJV)*

"FREE AT LAST!"

Slavery is a practice in which people own other people. Slavery began in prehistoric times and has been practiced ever since. The enslavement of blacks in the American Colonies began during the 1600's. Slavery played a major role in the economic development of the United States. The American Slave Trade was a lucrative one for those who owned slaves. For the slave however, it was another story. Slaves were subjected to the cruelest tortures. They were hung, burned at the stake, dismembered, raped, castrated, and branded. All of these were done in addition to the usual whippings for even the smallest infractions.

Alex Haley was an American Author who became famous for his book *"Roots: The Saga Of An American Family"* **(1976)**. In his book, Haley combined fact and fiction as he described the history of his family beginning in the mid 1700's in Africa. *"Roots"* follows the struggle of Haley's family in America as slaves and later as free people. He spent 12 years researching *"Roots."* His book was later turned into an eight –part dramatization which appeared on television in the U.S. in 1977 (*10). The images of slavery that emanated from my television screen will forever be "etched" in my memory banks! Reading and hearing about the atrocities of slavery is one thing. Seeing them is another. The same rings true for the Holocaust. The Holocaust was the mass murder of the European Jews by the Nazis during World War I. I well remember sitting in my history classes as the film projector showed the graphic and horrific images of what Nazi Dictator Adolph Hitler did to six million Jews. Millions of Jews were imprisoned in concentration camps. The camps had gas chambers that were used to kill a massive amount of victims. The camps also had factories in which prisoners were worked to death. The captives lived under horrible conditions and many died of starvation and disease.

Doctors were permitted to perform cruel experiments on some prisoners (*10). The enslavement of Blacks and the mass murder of six million Jews, are terrible events marking low and dark periods in America's history. The setting free of slaves with the North's victory over the South in the Civil War, and the defeat of Hitler in World War I, brought an end to the pains of "bondage" for Blacks and Jews. Although liberated physically, the emotional, social, and economic "wounds" suffered by both races, were carried into future generations. These "wounds," I'm afraid, have never truly healed.

Can you imagine what the slaves and the people in the concentration camps had to endure on a daily basis? These people were innocent. They hadn't done anything wrong to deserve their punishment and abuse. They were simply victims of circumstance. But for the grace of God, there go we. I could never imagine being taken from my home against my will and subjected to horrendous torture. The mere thought of it is too frightening for words! For those who had the experience and went through it however, know it to be a harsh reality. Most of us Christians may not be able to testify about "physical" bondage to a great extent, but we sure can tell of the "spiritual" bondage to sin we have endured. All of us were born in sin and shaped in iniquity. No matter how "morally" good one tries to live and be, it won't get rid of the sin nature inherited from Adam. Romans 5:12 states: *"Wherefore, as by one man sin entered the world, and death by sin; and so death passed upon all men, for that all have sinned:" (KJV)* What can wash away my sins? Nothing but the blood of Jesus! Until a person accepts him as their Lord and personal Savior, they are a "slave" to sin under the influence and mastery of Satan. I John 3:8 reads as thus: *"He that committeth sin is of the devil; for the devil sinneth from the beginning. For this purpose the Son of God was manifested, that he might destroy the works of the devil."(KJV)* If a person rejects Christ and dies in their sins, hell will be that person's eternal resting place. Many people often ask the question, what is sin? Sin simply means missing the "mark" by not living up to God's holy and righteous standard. We commit sin when we break God's laws. There aren't any so called "big" sins or "little" sins in God's eyesight. The Bible says, *"All unrighteousness is sin." (I John 5:17 KJV)* Every one of us has missed the "mark" and fallen short of God's expectation of us. *"For all have sinned and fallen short of the Glory of God." (Romans 3:23 KJV)* How many of us will honestly admit that even after receiving Jesus Christ as our Lord and Personal Savior, we have been found guilty of missing the "mark" and done things we should not have done? Thank God for His Grace and Mercy! Ephesians 2:8 reads as thus: *"For by grace are ye saved through faith; and that not of yourselves: it is the gift of God:"(KJV)* Jeremiah 3:22-23 states: *"It is the Lord's mercies that we are not consumed, because his compassions fail not. They are new every morning: great is thy faithfulness."(KJV)* None of us can ever think that "we have arrived" or dotted every "I" and crossed every "T." Sanctification is an ongoing process for *all* Christians ending the day we close our eyes in death. Sin has a way of enslaving people, controlling them, dominating them and dictating their actions. There are many many aspects of "bondage" and it has many faces. **Drug addiction, alcoholism, sex addiction, perversion, pornography, over eating/poor diet, smoking, adultery, fornication, depression, materialism, idolatry, coveting, meanness, insensitiveness, gossiping, laziness, rudeness, mental illness, stealing, lying, anger, lust, jealousy/envy, unforgiveness, fear, hatred, pride, the past, selfishness, bitterness, vengeance, etc.,** are just some of the things "gripping" people holding them captive making them servants of Satan. Another area of "bondage" that we have to be aware of is bondage to "people." Being "enslaved" to the persuading opinions others have about us. We must be delivered from the **"what others will think of me"** attitude. They want to control you by telling you what *"they"* think you should wear, buy, and drive. How they think you should talk and conduct yourself.

They even decide who your friends should be. How you should live your life. What to do with your spiritual gift, and so on. We are commanded by God to obey His voice. Listening to "people" instead of God will ruin your life forever! "Bondage" in any form will keep you from becoming the person God created you to be. There is no person or thing worth you going to hell over! Get rid of sin before sin gets rid of you!

What's the cure? **JESUS!** If sin is restraining, mastering, or enslaving you, Jesus can break its power over your life! Jesus cares about the whole "man." He heals our "physical" and "spiritual" wounds. There are countless Christians who were in the same situation, in "bondage" to sin. It wasn't until a loving Jesus chose us and called us out of sin that we could be freed from it's handcuffs. No matter how hard we tried on our own to stop the sinful and destructive practices, we could not give them up. Satan had us right where he wanted us, on the downward road straight to hell. But thank God for Jesus! He did a complete work in us. He washed us clean with His precious blood and filled us with His Spirit to enable us to live this new life of spiritual freedom. And when the time comes for us to close our eyes in death, in Heaven we will be for eternity, joyously fellowshipping with the **TRINITY!** What a glorious time that'll be! With the Devil, there was guilt, condemnation, bitterness, and sadness. With my Lord Jesus, there is hope, love, joy, peace, and gladness! The Son has made a way for us to be free! We can't do it on our own and we don't have to. You don't have to remain in the bondage of "sin," for Jesus' loving arms will gladly take you in. I'm a witness! The Devil will tell you all sorts of lies about you not being able to come out of whatever you may be in. Just remember, he is a liar and the *TRUTH* is not in him! You may feel that there is no hope for you and whatever has you bound is going to take you out. I want you to know that there is no sin that Jesus can't deliver us from! There is no sin that is greater, stronger or more powerful than God's love! All we have to do is ask him for deliverance and believe by faith that it is done. Faith is not believing that God *CAN* do it. Faith is knowing that God has already *DONE* it!

"I'm Free,"
"Praise the Lord I'm Free."
"No longer bound,"
"No more chains holding me,"
"My soul is resting,"
"It's just a blessing,"
"Praise the Lord, Hallelujah I'm Free!"

(Congregational Song. Author unknown)

Chapter 12

"Born Again"

Born Again – New birth. (*5)

New Birth – The technical expression frequently used for regeneration, which is the spiritual change wrought in man as a result of having been born of water and of the Spirit. (*5)

Regeneration – The change wrought in the thought, feeling, and will of man, in his relation to God and the world. The instrument which God uses to bring regeneration is his word (I Thess. 2:13). This "new birth" is outwardly symbolized by baptism. (*5)

Fact – There are many who believe that simply going to Church and acting "religious" makes one a righteous person. Others feel since they are related to the Pastor or some ordained officer of the Church, they are therefore more righteous and more important than those who do not share their DNA, family name, and pedigree.

TRUTH – *"Jesus answered and said unto him, verily, verily, I say unto thee, except a man be born again, he cannot see the kingdom of God." Except a man be born of water and of the Spirit he cannot enter into the kingdom of God." (John 3:3 & 5 KJV)*

TRUTH – *"Being born again, not of corruptible seed but of incorruptible, by the word of God which liveth and abideth for ever."* *(1 Peter 1:23 KJV)*

TRUTH – *"For I will take you from among the heathen, and gather you out of all countries, and will bring you into your own land. Then will I sprinkle clean water upon you, and ye shall be clean: from all your filthiness, and from all your idols, will I cleanse you. A "new" heart also will I give you, and a new "spirit" will I put within you: and I will take away the stony heart out of your flesh, and I will give you an heart of flesh. And I will put my Spirit within you, and cause you to walk in my statutes, and ye shall keep my judgments and do them."* *(Ezekiel 36: 24–27 KJV)*

"FROM RELIGION TO RELATIONSHIP, FROM TRADITION TO TESTIMONY"

There is a big difference between "guess so" salvation and "know so" salvation. There is a big difference between "church" membership and being a member of "God's" Church. There is a big difference between having a "form" of godliness but denying the power thereof and having the "power" of God working in your life. The mark of distinction for one having "know so" salvation, being a member of "God's" Church, and having the "power" of God working in your life is the *"Born Again"* experience.

It can't be imitated, duplicated, or fabricated, by "man." Either you have it or you don't. It's that simple! Without the "born again" experience, one is literally a religious person performing routine acts of worship. The individual may be a faithful, sincere, fervent person working in the "church" but this is no indication that, that individual's heart has been changed by God. Coming to church doesn't make one "born again." Many people go to church for various reasons. Most of which however, have nothing to do with "salvation." For some, it is "tradition." For as long as they can remember, going to church on Sunday was the routine. For others, they go out of obligation. "My parents make me go." "I'm an officer of the church so I have to be present." Others see church as a place to gather for social events. It's a good place to search for a mate or significant other. A place to get married, christened, and buried. A place to go on outings, picnics, trips. A great place to leave your children when you need to take some time for yourself. A great place for networking. Others have clout, status and influence there. The list of reasons is a long one. Very few people go to church because they "genuinely" love the Lord and strive to have a deeper personal relationship with him. Most can tell you the day they "joined" the church but they can't tell you when they were "converted." By converted I mean having a personal encounter with Jesus resulting in a complete turn from a worldly way of life (and all of the sinful passions and pleasures that go along with it), to a new life of spiritual holiness. A sincere passion and desire for God and righteous things will become the ultimate aim. Glorifying God will now be the top priority. This is where the problem lies. Churches nowadays are largely made up of those who have the "form" but no power to "transform." They would rather "perform" than "conform" to God and walk in the Spirit! They are "busy bees," so preoccupied with working *for the Lord,* they don't even realize that they are not doing the work *of the Lord!* They do a lot of things except manifest maturity in Christ. Outwardly, they appear to be living obedient lives to God. Inwardly however, there has been no spiritual renewal. They keep up appearances by doing a lot of religious works. They think their busyness is what makes them spiritual and righteous. Sad to say, most never truly reach their full potential in God by being and doing what *He* wants them to. Because of this, many churches have "cooled" off spiritually from the church of yester year. The congregations are now largely made up of "complacent", "burned" out Christians instead of "growing," "on fire" Christians." There are a lot of "emotionally" charged services being held, but no real "spiritual" heat is manifested. This is nothing new of course. During Jesus' day the Pharisees were a group of Jewish people who zealously followed Old Testament law as well as their own traditions. They were guilty of adding hundreds of religious traditions to God's law and considered them all equally important. The Pharisees were highly respected in the community, but they hated Jesus because he challenged their proud attitudes and dishonorable motives. The Pharisees had placed their laws above human need (*4). They were Bible scholars, pious, and religious, but they lacked one main thing, they had no relationship with *Christ.* No relationship with him means no conversion! The Apostle Paul is a great example from the Bible of a Pharisee that Christ takes from **"Religion to relationship and from tradition to testimony."**

A Jew by birth, he was born a few years after the birth of Jesus in the city of Tarsus. His original name was Saul. As a youth, Paul went to Jerusalem and studied under the famous rabbi Gamaliel. Paul was very religious. At this time, he believed deeply in Judaism. His intentions and efforts were sincere. In Jerusalem, Paul met Jews who had become Christians. They believed Jesus, who recently had been crucified, was the Messiah, the promised Savior of the Jews. Paul zealously began to persecute these Jews because their views and behavior offended him (*4 & *10). But one day, while traveling to Damascus, his life would be changed forever. *"And as he journeyed, he came near Damascus: and suddenly there shined round about him a light from heaven: and he fell to the earth, and heard a voice saying unto him, Saul, Saul, why persecutest thou me? And he said, Who art thou, Lord? And the Lord said, I am Jesus whom thou persecutest: it is hard for thee to kick against the pricks. And he trembling and astonished said, Lord, what wilt thou have me to do? And the Lord said unto him, arise, and go into the city, and it shall be told thee what thou must do."(KJV)* Saul had a one on one encounter with the risen Christ. He became face to face with the truth of the Gospel. He was a changed man from that day forth! Saul goes three days without food or drink. This, in addition to the shock of his exposure to the resurrected Christ, left him weak. However, several things helped him regain his strength: his encounter with Ananias, his healing, his filling with the Spirit, his water baptism, and his taking some food. Saul the persecutor was about to become Paul the apostle of Jesus Christ! His background and qualifications suited him eminently for the work to which God had called him: 1) He knew the Jewish culture and language well. 2) He was reared in Tarsus and was well acquainted with the Greek culture and its philosophies. 3) He possessed all the privileges of a Roman citizen. 4) He was trained and skilled in Jewish theology. 5) He was capable in a secular trade and was able to support himself. 6) God gave him zeal, leadership qualities, and theological insight (*2). Just think, he had gone to Damascus to persecute the church; he ended up preaching Jesus! After only a few days with the Christians in Damascus, Saul began to preach in the synagogues that Jesus is the Son of God. There was no doubt to those around him that a change had been made in his life. Acts 9:21 states: ***"But all that heard him were amazed, and said; is not this he that destroyed them which called on this name (Jesus) in Jerusalem, and came hither for that intent, that he might bring them bound unto the chief priests?"(KJV)*** Paul goes on to be one of the most important leaders of early Christianity. He became the apostle to the Gentiles and a world traveler for Christ. The thorny issue of whether Gentile believers had to obey Jewish laws before they could become Christians caused many problems in the early church. Paul worked hard to convince the Jews that Gentiles were acceptable to God, but he spent even more time convincing the Gentiles that they were acceptable to God (*4). By means of his letters, Paul encouraged early Christians as well as modern day Christians in times of discouragement and persecution. He reminded his followers of their responsibilities to one another and thus provided many basic ideas of Christianity. His letters are a central part of the New Testament.

The Apostle Paul's life is a wonderful example of what can happen in the life of a *"**Born Again**"* believer! His story proves that God can save anybody he wants to! When you have had an encounter with the Master, you cannot remain the same. The things you used to do, the places you used to go, and people you used to know, will all be a thing of the past. This is your testimony! You can tell others how your life has changed. Paul became a witness for Christ as soon as his strength returned and he was on his feet again. When you are "born again," the purpose for your life and what God wants you to do will be revealed to you. You will have a new direction and calling in life that no amount of persecution or opposition can stop. God will place a "spiritual" fire in you that will compel and propel you to do His command. This new direction and calling will not be done out of obligation, religious, or traditional reasons. It will freely and gladly be done because you know beyond a shadow of a doubt that God has wrought a mighty change in you! He has graciously and mercifully taken you from **"Religion to relationship and from tradition to testimony!**

"Have you been to Jesus for the cleansing pow'r?"
"Are you washed in the blood of the Lamb?"
"Are you fully trusting in His grace this hour?"
"Are you washed in the blood of the Lamb"
"Are you washed"
"In the blood,"
"In the soul cleansing blood of the Lamb?"
"Are your garments spotless?"
"Are they white as snow?"
"Are you washed in the blood of the Lamb?"

*(Hymn by Elisha A. Hoffman *6)*

Chapter 13

"Charity"

Charity – Love of one's fellow man. God's love to man. (*9)

Love – The kindly feeling or benevolence of God for his creatures; the reverent devotion due from them to God; the kindly affection they should have for each other. (*9)

Sacrifice – The act of giving up one thing for another, destruction or surrender of something valued or desired for the sake of a higher object or more pressing claim. To permit injury or disadvantage to, for the sake of something else. (*9)

Share – To use together; enjoy together, have in common. To divide into parts, each taking a part. Participate, partake, to use, enjoy, or have something in common with another. Joining with others in some activity or undertaking. (*9)

Fact – You will be surprised by what "little" acts of kindness are capable of accomplishing. Though slowly diminishing in our modern and contemporary culture, acts of kindness can and do go a long way.

TRUTH – *"Jesus said unto him, Thou shalt love the Lord thy God with all thy heart, soul, and with all thy mind. This is the first and great commandment. And the second*

is like unto it, Thou shalt love thy neighbor as thyself."
(Matthew 22:37-39 KJV)

TRUTH – *"For God so loved the world, that he gave his only begotten Son, that whosoever believeth in him should not perish but have everlasting life." (John 3:16 KJV)*

TRUTH – *"And now abideth faith, hope, charity, these three; but the greatest of these is charity." (I Corinthians 13:13 KJV)*

"LET GO WHAT YOU GOT, AND WATCH GOD GIVE YOU MORE!"

Teaching little children how to share has to be one of the toughest principles most parents find imparting to their children. Most of us who have siblings know and remember all too well what it was like growing up with our brothers and sisters at times. I'm sure you well remember that favorite toy, article of clothing, money, favorite food, etc., you had growing up. If you were like me, you didn't want anyone to look at it, let alone have it! As soon as we saw someone coming, we would either hide it, or quickly eat it so that we wouldn't have to part with it. Are some of us still a little guilty of this today? Love is not supposed to act this way.

Thank God for Godly parents and teachers. Their role was that of mediator. They stepped in to correct and instruct us as to the proper way of dealing with selfishness. We must remember that love is the most important virtue in the Christian life. The impartation of spiritual lessons and principles to the heart of a child while he or she is young is vitally important. What we learn and how we develop as a child will carry behavior patterns right into adulthood. _**"A man's harvest in life is a direct result of the seeds he has sown."**_ Is there a benefit to not being selfish? Can we gain more by letting go what we have sometimes and giving to others? What about in times of lack or shortage? What is the benefit of me _**"letting go what I got"**_ when I don't even have enough for myself? The latter question is hard on the **"flesh."** We as Christians are reminded in Romans 8:4b _**"That the righteousness of the law might be fulfilled in us, who walk not after the flesh, but after the Spirit."(KJV)**_ The Bible has many examples of those who walked after the "Spirit" and exercised their faith to "let go what they had." Their surrender and submission to God's will, allowed Him to bless them with more than they ever could have imagined. Their stories can serve as valuable learning tools and lessons of great faith to inspire us all to do better in the area of self sacrifice.

Our first example from the Bible comes from I Kings chapter 17. The prophet Elijah prophesied a drought and then hid from King Ahab by the Cherith Brook. While there, Elijah was fed by ravens. It's truly amazing how the animal kingdom obeys God better than us humans at times, but that's another lesson. When the brook dried up, God sent Elijah to Zarephath in Phonecia, where a widow and her son lived. Verses 10-16 states *"So he arose and went to Zarephath, and when he came to the gate of the city, behold the widow woman was there gathering sticks: and he called to her, and said, fetch me, I pray thee a little water in a vessel, that I may drink. And as she was going to fetch it, he called to her, and said, bring me, I pray thee, a morsel of bread in thine hand. And she said, as the Lord thy God liveth, I have not a cake, but a <u>handful</u> of meal in a barrel, and a little oil in a cruse: and behold, I am getting two sticks, that I may go and dress it for me and my son, that we may eat it and die. And Elijah said unto her, fear not; go and do as thou hast said: but make me thereof a little cake <u>first</u>, and bring it unto <u>me</u>, and after make for thee and for thy son. For thus saith the Lord God of Israel, the barrel of meal shall not waste, neither shall the cruse of oil fail, until the day the Lord sendeth rain upon the earth. <u>And she went and did according to the saying of Elijah:</u> and she, and he and her house did eat <u>many days.</u> And the barrel of meal wasted not, neither did the cruse of oil fail, <u>according to the word of the Lord, which he spake by Elijah."(KJV)</u>*

This is a wonderful example of someone having love and faith to **"let go what they had,"** allowing God to bless them with more! If this woman had been selfish and only concerned about her own needs, she and her son most assuredly would have died. She thought she was preparing her last meal. Her simple act of faith produced a miracle.

Faith is "believing without seeing." To the natural eye, the situation seemed hopeless. This woman looked beyond her "natural" sight and grabbed a hold of her "spiritual" sight. Every miracle, large or small, begins with an act of **obedience.** Obedience is a test of love (John 14:15). Is there anything too hard for God? NO! Bishop Forbes always tells his members, *"You can't beat God giving."* I'm a witness, you can't. Later in this chapter, the widow's son dies. Elijah prays to God that the child's spirit will be returned to him and the Lord honors the petition. Verse 24 states, *"And the woman said to Elijah, now by this I know that thou art a man of God, and that the word of the Lord in thy mouth is truth."(KJV)* When we walk in love and obedience and **"let go what we got,"** this gives the Lord the opportunity to come in and bless us! When this happens, others, especially the *unsaved* will see it and God's name will get the glory!

Our next example is of a child who was willing to "let go what he had" so God could give more. It is in the 6th chapter of John where we find the feeding of the 5,000. After Jesus crossed over the Sea of Galilee, He was followed by a huge crowd on their way to Jerusalem for the annual Passover celebration. These people followed Jesus wherever He went to watch Him heal the sick. Jesus turned to Philip and asked him where could they buy bread? Philip replied that it would take a fortune to do it. Then Andrew spoke up and said, *"There is a lad here, which hath five barley loaves, and two small fishes: but what are they among so many?(KJV)* Jesus took the loaves and gave thanks to God and passed them out to the people. Afterwards, He did the same with the fish. Everyone present ate until full. Twelve baskets were filled with leftovers! The disciples are contrasted with the child who was willing to "let go what he had." The disciples I'm sure had more resources than the lad did. Since they didn't have **enough,** they decided not to give anything at all. Love is a test of discipleship. John 13:35 states: *"By this shall all men know that ye are my disciples, if ye have love one to another."(KJV)* The lad gave what little he had and it made all the difference. If we offer nothing to God, he won't have anything to work with. Once we learn how to **"put our insufficiency into the hands of an all sufficient God,"** He will take it and multiply it for His glory! Age does not make a difference with God. We can learn a lot from children. God used what a young child offered in love to accomplish one of the greatest miracles recorded in the gospels.

So what are some of the things you may be holding on to instead of "letting go?" Are you failing to tithe because you don't see how you can afford to do it? What about your spiritual gift or talent? Are you holding on to it because you believe your gift is "small" and "insignificant" and could never be of help to someone else? What about your time? How much of it does God get? Let go of negative sinful things and watch God give you positive righteous things. Let go of hate and watch God give you Love. Let go of Fear and watch God give you Faith! You don't know what the Lord can do in and through your life if you walk in love and obedience to him. Remember, we reap what we sow. If we sow sparingly, we will reap sparingly. We are blessed to be a blessing to others. "Let go what you got, and watch what God will do with it! You will never be sorry you did!

"I was sinking deep in sin,"
"Far from the peaceful shore,"
"Very deeply stained within,"
"Sinking to rise no more;"
"But the Master of the sea"
"Heard my despairing cry,"
"From the waters lifted me"
"Now safe am I."
"Love lifted me, Love lifted me,"
"When nothing else could help,"
"Love lifted me."

*(Hymn by James Rowe *6)*

Chapter 14

"Compromise"

Compromise – A concession or yielding to something derogatory or prejudicial. To make shameful or disreputable granting. (*8 & *9)

Conviction – Certainty; assurance. The fact or condition of being convinced of one's sin. (*9)

Integrity – Honesty or sincerity. Uprightness. Undivided or unbroken condition; completeness, wholeness, perfect condition; soundness. Incorruptibility. (*8)

Fact – Compromising your integrity is <u>not</u> hard to do. Maintaining it <u>is!</u>

TRUTH – *"And be not conformed to this world: but be ye transformed by the renewing of your mind, that you may prove what is that good, and acceptable, and perfect, will of God." (Romans 12:2 KJV)*

"HOW IS YOUR INTEGRITY TODAY?"

Are you a person of conviction or compromise? Are you a person marked by "distinction" or "disguise?" Christians are faced with many tough challenges that test our witness and resolve for God. One of the biggest challenges facing many of us today is in the area of **_compromise._** How are the Saints of God expected to maintain our stance and integrity for God when we are constantly being bombarded by the daily solicitations, allurements and trappings of the world?

Churches are filled Sunday after Sunday with countless people professing their love, fidelity, and allegiance to Christ. While in the church setting, the commitment to God seems unshakeable, unbreakable, and unmovable. Away from the church however, is another story. The Bible reminds us *"we are in the world but not of it."* This simply means that "outwardly" we are a part of the world system but not "inwardly." We are a "redeemed" people set apart from the world for the Master's use. *Knowing* Godly Principles is one thing. *Living them* in the midst of a crooked and perverse generation is where the real challenge lies. The images we see, things we hear, conversations we are a part of, company we keep, etc, all impact us in profound ways. The grass always looks a little "greener" on the other side of the fence. How do we maintain our Christian Principles and convictions without compromising them in order to be accepted by the world? How do we consistently do *right* when *wrong* is all around us? How do we persist to do *good* when *evil* presses in on us and the desire to do the wrong thing at times seems to come so naturally? There is a constant battle for balance and contentment with what God has given us. On the one hand, we're striving to maintain our integrity without being "absorbed" or "conformed" by our modern day culture's influences and lifestyles. While at the same time, we must not be found guilty of isolating ourselves from others harboring critical, judgmental and self-righteous views against them. Jesus commands us to be both **"salt"** and **"light"** to the world. We certainly can't accomplish this by "withdrawing" ourselves from the unsaved. This is the great **"paradox,"** **"quandary,"** **"dilemma"** which perplexes God's people. This dilemma is marked by trial, pressure, and difficulty. Should I be a person of *"distinction"* and "go against the grain," "swim against the flow of the river," "upset the applecart?" Or should I be a person of *"disguise"* and simply put my Christian beliefs aside and be a part of the "status quo?" After all, it is much easier to "go with the flow of the river" or "when in Rome do as the Romans do." Besides, it costs too much nowadays to be a person of distinction. There is no real prize in "daring to be different." True Saints of God know the voice of Satan, when they hear it. We know for certain that there is one thing we cannot afford to do and that is **_compromise!_** Maintaining our integrity is priceless and will pay off in more ways than we can ever imagine.

As I stated earlier, living the "Christian" life around the Saints on Sundays is no great challenge. How effective is our witness and stance for Christ Monday through Saturday when we find ourselves among the unsaved at work, in school, while shopping, on vacation, etc. Are we still able to maintain our integrity when no one around us believes as we do and we are forced to be the "minority" when it comes to living as a Christian ought? Do we become "closet" Christians "blending in" with everyone else having no true witness for Christ? What do you; the eight year old do when you are walking home from school and the friend you are walking home with decides to steal candy from the candy store? Do you eat some of the candy and make plans to do it again the next day or do you do what your Mom and Dad told you to do and tell someone? What do you; the saved teenager do, when you hear that there is going to be a secret party at the captain of the football team's house while his parents are out of town. Everyone who's anyone is going! "Be there or be square" is the motto voiced in the hallways between classes. You know for a fact that alcohol will be served there. Your best friend wants to go and won't go without you. They carefully come up with a plan for you. They want you to tell your parents that you'll be spending the night at their house. This is partially true. You will be spending the night but after the party of course. Your best friend knows you are a Christian and has come to Church with you on several occasions. Their question to you is this: ***"Can't you just bend your stupid rules for once?"*** Which way do you turn? Do you compromise your beliefs and go along knowing it is wrong to do, or do you maintain your convictions and do the right thing? What do you; the saved college student do, when the answers to a very tough final exam for your Biochemistry Class have been stolen by a fellow student. This class has challenged you all semester and passing the final with an "A" would give you the G.P.A. needed to make the Dean's List. What do you do? Everyone in class is geared up for the final now that they have all the answers. Are you going to be a person of "distinction" or are you going to "drop your religion" like a hot potato and cheat as well? Let's not leave out the adults. Have you, the saved adult, ever told or laughed at an "off colored" joke? Have you ever been given too much change by a cashier and kept the money calling it a "blessing" from the Lord? Have you ever gossiped at the water cooler about a fellow co-worker? Would you do **_whatever_** it takes both fair and unfair, in order to receive a raise or promotion at work? Have you not spoken to someone you normally speak to because the people you happen to be around at the time don't like that person? What about that company Christmas Party last year? Did you partake of alcoholic beverages so as not to "stand out" from everyone else? Do you play the lottery or go to casinos with hopes of winning the "big one" as opposed to being a faithful tither to your church? At tax time, do you tell "little" white lies about your financial position in order to receive larger refunds allowing you to give substantial donations each year to your Pastor for his Anniversary? If Christ were to walk through your office, school, house, or neighborhood on any given day of the week, would He have trouble identifying you as a follower of His because of your style of dress, conversation, conduct and behavior?

These are just a few examples of the many ways we can so easily compromise our beliefs when we find ourselves placed in a precarious situation. Talking the talk is one thing, walking the walk is another! I know for certain I have come short of the Glory of God by failing to live up to my Christian Principles and beliefs at times. And I'm sure if you are honest with yourself, you have as well. We let the fear of *"what others will think of me,"* cause us to lower our standards. Thank God for His awesome grace and mercy extended towards us. If it were left up to justice, all of us would have been cut off a long time ago. It is vitally important for us Christians to maintain our witness and resolve for Christ. A charge to keep we have and a God to glorify. We must and have to do what is right at all times because we represent God here on earth. It is His holy and righteous standard that we must uphold. God's name is to be glorified and magnified. When we the servants of His lower the standard by committing all types of ungodly sins, we give the unsaved ammunition against the church. We put God in a bad light making Him appear to be weak. Because of our shortcomings, God's name becomes profane among the unsaved giving them an excuse for not living righteously. We have to lift up the blood stained banner for Christ. If the Christians don't do it then who will? Modern day Saints here in the West are not being put to death for being a follower of Christ. Most of us can't even stand being ostracized and ridiculed for our Faith. Dying for it for most, would definitely be out of the question. As I write these words, I'm reminded of some key examples from the Bible of those who even on pangs of death, courageously maintained their resolve and witness for God.

First there is my favorite Bible character Joseph. At the tender age of seventeen we find him being betrayed by his brothers, separated from his dear father, sold into slavery, ending up in Potipher's house. He does well there until he finds himself being sexually harassed by Potipher's wife. Holding fast to his faith, he purposes in his heart not to sin against God by refusing to enjoy the "pleasures of sin for a season." Daniel prayed in spite of the King's direct decree not to do so, was willing to face hungry lions rather than turn his back on God. The three Hebrew Boys standing _**tall**_ in defiance against King Nebuchadnezzar's decree to _**bow**_. Willing to face a fiery furnace for refusing to "dance" to anyone's music except the Lord's! God honored and greatly rewarded these and other heroes of the Bible _**mightily**_ for their uncompromising resolve to serve him. Since none of us know where life is going to take us, we need to gain all the Faith and encouragement from their example we can. We have to be ready when the "test" to compromise our integrity is given to us. Rest assured, the _**TESTS**_ will come. The question is, will we pass them? Don't side with the world. Be a rebel _**"with a cause."**_ What cause; some will ask you. Your reply, _**"For the cause of Christ, I am what I am and I believe what I believe!"**_ God's greatest blessing awaits those of us who purpose in our heart to maintain our integrity no matter the cost. Doing the right thing always pays off in more ways than we know or will ever be able to imagine. How do we know this for sure? The Bible tells us so....

"I don't possess houses or lands, fine clothes or jewelry,"
"Sorrow and cares, in this old world my lot seems to be,"
"But I have a Christ, all in my life, this makes me happy,"
"For Christ is all, all and all, this world to me."

**(Hymn by Kenneth Morris *6)**

Chapter 15

"Contend"

Contend – To work hard against difficulties, opposition; fight; struggle. (*9)

Press – To seek urgently; contend. To force or push one's way. (*9)

Pressure – The burden of physical or mental distress. (*9)

Fact – Life for the Christian gets hard at times. If we can't make it through the "small" difficulties that arise, then we will have an even tougher time making it through the "larger" ones.

TRUTH – *"If thou hast run with the footmen, and they have wearied thee, then how canst thou <u>contend</u> with horses?" (Jeremiah 12:5 KJV)*

TRUTH – *"Thou therefore endure hardness, as a good soldier of Jesus Christ." (II Timothy 2:3 KJV)*

TRUTH - *"I count not myself to have apprehended, but this one thing I do; forgetting those things which are behind, I <u>press</u> toward the mark for the prize of the high calling of God."(Philippians 3:13-14 KJV)*

"PRESS YOUR WAY!"

As we begin each day afresh, we may not know what the future holds for that day, but we do know who holds the future! The Christian journey for many of us has been marked by great trial, struggle, and constant pressure. Satan has definitely heightened his level of attack against God's people. Long have been the nights, high have been the mountains, and low have been the valleys! No one told us the journey would be easy, but they didn't tell us just how tough it would be at times either. In the words of the famous gospel singer Mahailia Jackson, ***"My soul looks back and wonders how I got over!"*** We are in the fight of our lives. Make sure you put your full armor on each and every day! Don't leave home without it! We are commanded by God to be ***"Good Soldiers"*** in His ***"Salvation Army."*** This battle is serious and should not be taken lightly. Our soul is what's at stake here. Where will we spend eternity? Nothing more can be done or added to "yesterday." That chapter of our lives is closed forever. Whatever mistakes were made, whatever was or wasn't done, can't be fixed now. Pray about it, learn from it, forget about it, and press on! That's what the Apostle Paul did. We can't allow anything to stop us from reaching the high call of God! As I write these words, my soul is flooded with so many great examples from the Bible of those who had to "press their way" and contend for the faith. Their stories offer hope, courage, and inspiration to us as we too, ***"press our way"*** along this pilgrim journey.

It is in Luke 15:11-32 where we find Jesus telling the parable of the lost son. This parable shows the joy of those who "press their way" to repentance. In the parable, a certain man had two sons. One day, the younger son comes to his father and asks for his portion of the inheritance. The father honors the request and the young man gathers all his belongings and leaves home. He goes into a far country and squanders all of his money on worldly pleasures. Soon after, a famine hits the land and the young man becomes destitute. He finds a job feeding swine and is so hungry he wants to eat the pigs food. According to Moses' law, pigs were unclean animals. This meant they could not be eaten or used for sacrifices. To protect themselves from defilement, Jews would not even touch them. For a Jew to stoop and feed them was bad enough. But to eat the pigs food was the lowest any Jew could fall to. He truly had reached rock bottom! He did not receive help from anyone. He was completely alone. What happened to all of those *"friends"* he had which helped him waste his money? They disappeared when the *"wine,"* *"women,"* and *"song"* ended! What did the young man do? Verses 17-20 tell us. *"And when he came to himself, he said, how many hired servants of my father's have bread enough and to spare, and I perish with hunger! I will arise and go to my father, and will say unto him, Father, I have sinned against heaven, and before thee, and am no more worthy to be called thy son: make me as one of thy hired servants. And he arose, and came to his father. But when he was yet a great way off, his father saw him, and had <u>compassion</u>, ran, and fell on his neck, and kissed him."(KJV)* Conversion for this young man took place when he made up in his mind to return home. He repented, confessed and turned from his evil way. His heart was in the right spiritual position (contrite) to receive his father's forgiveness. When he returned home, this was his "public" demonstration that he had been converted and was ready to begin a "new" life of faith and obedience.

This parable depicts the awesome love and forgiveness that God has for sinners. The *"Prodigal Son"* had to *"press his way"* and forget about his pride, his past failures, mistakes, and most of all, what others would think about him. He needed his father and that's all that mattered. It is interesting to note that the young man's biggest critic was his very own "blood brother." He was unforgiving and bitter. If anyone had a right to complain about the young man's actions, it was his father. The father wasn't bitter. He was joyous! He forgave him and restored him back to his original position. When Jesus told this story, the older brother's attitude represented the **Pharisees,** who were angry and resentful that sinners were being welcomed in God's Kingdom. God forgives and forgets sin, people never do. There will always be Pharisees around waiting to point their self-righteous and judgmental finger at you to condemn you. They can clearly see everyone else's sins and shortcomings except their own. *"All have sinned and come short of the Glory of God."* All of us are in need of a Savior! Don't let what people say about you stop you from "pressing your way" to the high call of God! Don't allow your *"past"* to keep you from reaching your *"future!"* Learn to be a contender!

Our next example is also from the book of Luke. Luke 8:43-48 gives us the story of the woman with the issue of blood. She had been sick for twelve long years and spent all she had on doctors trying to find a cure for her. According to the law, she was considered "unclean" which made her an outcast to society. On this particular day, Jesus was in town healing people. As usual, there was a great crowd of people surrounding Jesus following Him. She shouldn't have been a part of the crowd in the first place, and definitely wasn't supposed to touch anyone. She knew the law plainly but decided to *"press her way"* anyway. Verses 43-46 reads as thus: *"And a woman having an issue of blood twelve years, which had spent all of her living upon physicians, neither could be healed of any, came behind him, and touched the border of his garment: and immediately her issue of blood stanched. And Jesus said, who touched me? When all denied, Peter and they that were with him said, Master, the multitude throng thee and press thee, and sayest thou, who touched me? And Jesus said, somebody hath touched me: for I perceive that virtue is gone out of me."* *(KJV)* Jesus knew the "touch" He received was not an ordinary touch. Someone had "pressed their way" to Him and stretched out in "faith" to receive their healing. The woman confesses that it was she who touched Jesus. She knew she had broken man's law but she moved in "faith" and not in "fear." She contended for her healing, anyway! Because of her "press," Jesus not only healed her but he made her whole. When sickness and disease attacks our bodies, we must do the same thing. We too must "press our way" to Jesus, the Master Healer. No matter how long the "test," learn how to "press!" No matter how badly "stressed," learn how to "press!" No matter how big the "mess," learn how to "press!"

There are countless other examples in the Bible of those who had to "press" to the prize of the high call of God. Jeremiah's life was extremely difficult despite his love for and obedience to God. When he called to God for relief, God's reply in effect was "if you think this is bad, how are you going to cope when it really gets tough?" Christianity involves not only great blessings but often great suffering too. God calls us to commitment, not to comfort. He promises to be with us through suffering and hardship, not to spare us from them (The Living Bible). Remember Jesus in the Garden of Gethsemane wrestling with the cup. He was there contending with the forces of hell on our behalf. He had to "press" his way through it in order to seal the eternal salvation of "man." Remember Hannah's prayer in the temple for a son. Remember Abraham and Sarah believing God's promise of a son even though they both were well stricken in years. The list goes on and on. Their stories are written to encourage us to "press our way" toward the mark for the prize of the high call of God! When the going gets tough, the tough get going! Remember, you will never win if you don't contend! You will never win if you too quickly give in! You can and you will make it if you don't give up! **Press your way!**

"I left my friends and kindred"
"Bound for the Promised Land,"
"The grace of God upon me,"
"The Bible in my hand,"
"In distant lands I trod,"
"Crying sinner come to God,"
"I'm on the battlefield for my Lord."
"I am on the battlefield for my Lord,"
"I'm on the battlefield for my Lord;"
"And I promised him that I"
"Would serve Him til I die."
"I'm on the battlefield for my Lord."

(Hymn by Sylvia Bell & E. V. Banks *6)

Chapter 16

"Courage"

Courage – Bravery; meeting danger without fear. Fearlessness. Heart, mind, and disposition are fixed. Moral strength that makes a person face any danger, trouble, or pain steadily and without showing fear. Valiant, dauntless, heroic, daring, bold (*9)

Virtue – Moral excellence; goodness, uprightness, integrity. (*9)

Fact – When one hears the word "courage" he generally does not ascribe it as a characteristic usually found in women. "Courage" is perceived by most to be a trait only capable of being demonstrated by men.

Memory Selection: (Serenity Prayer) - *"God grant me the serenity to accept the things I cannot change: the courage to change the things I can: and the wisdom to know the difference."*

TRUTH – *"Be strong and of a good courage, fear not, nor be afraid of them; for the Lord thy God, he it is that doth go with thee; he will not fail thee, nor forsake thee." (Deuteronomy 31:6 KJV)*

"THE COURAGE OF ONE WOMAN"

Courage is the one characteristic each of us possesses in some form or another. Courage can't be determined or measured by a person's gender, age, race, physical appearance, educational background, economic standing or family name. The little shepherd boy David is a great example of this. To the natural eye, David was just a little kid who cared for a few sheep. David however, everyone quickly learns, possessed a "spiritual courage" that the natural eye could never see. His story lets me know to never underestimate anyone. It could be very costly.

Courage, although possessed by all is not always demonstrated by all. This does not mean however that you are not a courageous person. Many of us cannot know the true level of our courage until we are put to a strong and difficult test. We don't realize **the fight is in us** until **the war is on!** The famous poet Maya Angelou once wrote: *"Without courage, it is impossible to perform the other virtues."* There are seven virtues that each believer is to add to their faith. The list of virtues can be found in 2nd Peter 1: 5-7 and includes the following: **1) Goodness – This simply means Moral Excellency. 2) Knowledge – This type of knowledge comes not from intellectual pursuits, but is "spiritual" knowledge. 3) Self Control –This means to have one's passions under control. 4) Perseverance – "Staying under." It is frequently used in the New Testament to refer to constancy or steadfast endurance under adversity without giving in or giving up. 5) Godliness – Piety, man's obligation of reverence toward God. 6) Brotherly Kindness – The Greek word is "Philadelphian" where we get our American word "Philadelphia" from. Philadelphia is called the "City of**

Brotherly Love." Brotherly kindness is a fervent practical caring for others; concern for others' needs. 7) Love (Agapen) – It is desiring the <u>highest</u> good for others. This is the kind of love God exhibits toward sinners (*2). The first five virtues pertain to one's inner life and his relationship to God. The remaining two, relate to others. Queen Esther is a shining example to us of a courageous woman who demonstrated all seven of these virtues.

Esther's name means "star." She had been orphaned and subsequently adopted by her cousin Mordecai. Esther's story unfolds when Queen Vashti refuses to obey an order from her husband, King Ahasuerus. She is banished for her blatant act of disobedience and the search for a new queen begins. The King, in an attempt to find a new queen, sends out a decree to gather together all the beautiful women in the kingdom and bring them into the royal harem. Esther, a young Jewish woman, is chosen. Esther 2:17 states: *"And the king loved Esther above all women, and she obtained grace and favour in his sight more than all the virgins; so that he set the royal crown upon her head, and made her queen instead of Vashti."(KJV)* As Esther is being promoted, her cousin Mordecai foils an assassination plot against King Ahasuerus. Mordecai was not immediately rewarded for his kind deed. The king never knew anything about the incident. We Christians are reminded however that God may not come when you want Him, but He's always on time! In addition to Esther's appointment, Haman was also promoted by the king to be above all the princes that were with him. The king commanded all his servants to bow and reverence Haman. Mordecai bowed not nor did him reverence. He knew that this type of honor was to be given to God only. He did not compromise his religious beliefs to be accepted by man. Mordecai was not the only Jew around, he was the only Jew who chose to stand up for what was right. When Haman saw that Mordecai refused to bow to him, he became full of wrath. Because *one* Jew opposed him, he sought to destroy *all* the Jews. It is interesting to note that the Jews who **did bow** to Haman did not escape his hatred and evil intent. This shows me that going along with the crowd so you can "fit" in does not gain you anymore respect or "brownie points" from the person you are trying to please or cater to. We have two choices in life. We can either die standing up for what's right or live on our knees, not standing for anything. Mordecai chose to stand up!

Haman goes ahead with his plan to exterminate all Jews. He goes to the King and receives his permission to destroy them. Letters were then drafted and sent throughout the empire sealing the Jews fate. All Jews, both young and old, little children and women were to die on the 13th day of the twelfth month. The stage is now set for God and Esther to demonstrate the seven virtues I mentioned earlier. When Mordecai found out about the decree, He and many other Jews put on sackcloth with ashes. There was great mourning, wailing, and fasting among the Jews. Esther's maid and her Chamberlains come and tell her about Mordecai's behavior. Esther, in an act of ***goodness and brotherly kindness,*** sends one of her Chamberlains to Mordecai with a change of clothes and also to find out why he's so grieved and acting like he is. Notice Esther did not forget about her cousin and act like she did not know or remember him. Although she was Queen, living in a palace, wearing fine clothes, having the best material possessions, Mordecai was still her cousin. Sometimes when the Lord blesses us with material things, we forget about others who helped us along the way. Don't burn your bridges. You never know who you are going to need in life. Mordecai tells the Chamberlain about Haman's plot to kill the Jews and gives him a copy of the written decree. Mordecai instructs the Chamberlain to tell Esther to go to the King on the behalf of her people and ask that their lives be spared. Esther replies that there is a Persian Law stating a person can only come to the King's inner court if he has been summoned by the King. This person can be put to death unless the King holds out the golden scepter that he may live. Esther states she has not been called to come to the King in thirty days. Mordecai reminds Esther that she is Jewish also and stands the risk of being destroyed along with all of the other Jews if Haman's plan is allowed to come to pass. Notice Esther's demeanor. She displayed **_self control._** She did not panic, over react, or become hysterical over what Mordecai was asking her to do. How do you react when the pressure times show up in your life?

Esther's response to Mordecai was one of **_"spiritual knowledge" and godliness._** Chapter 4:16-17 reads: **_"Go, gather together all the Jews that are present in Shushan and fast ye for me, and neither eat nor drink three days, night or day: I also and my maidens will fast likewise; and so will I go unto the king, which is not according to the law: and if I perish, I perish."(KJV)_** The scriptures don't say they prayed. It is my heartfelt belief however, both fasting and praying were done for three days. Esther may not have been a regular attendee **_at_** the temple, but this test of faith shows what she had learned **_from_** the temple. She was able to draw from those things she had been taught when the testing time showed up! It should be the same way with us. Our focus should not be on how often we come **to church**. Our concern should be on what we are doing with that which we learn **from church**. The beginning of the 5th chapter of Esther finds her coming off her three day fast **bold** and **courageous!** Moving in **_perseverance_** and **_love,_** she goes to see the King. **_"Now it came to pass on the 3rd day, that Esther put on her royal apparel, and stood in the inner court of the king's house, over against the king's house: and the king sat upon his royal throne in the royal house...And it was so, when the king saw Esther the queen standing in the court, that she obtained favour in his sight: and the king held out to Esther the golden scepter that was in his hand. So Esther drew near, and touched the top of the scepter."(KJV)_**

The book of Esther closes on a victorious note! Esther reveals to the king Haman's evil plan to destroy her and her people. A second decree is written overturning the original one written by Haman. The Jews are given permission by the king to destroy those who sought to destroy them. Wicked Haman, who wanted to hang Mordecai on gallows he had constructed just for him, was hanged on it himself at the king's request. Be careful. You may fall into the very trap you have set for someone else. Remember we reap what we sow. What happens to Mordecai? The king finds out about Mordecai's kind deed which was never rewarded. He ultimately is promoted to the very position once held by his enemy Haman. ***"For Mordecai the Jew was next unto King Ahasuerus, and great among the Jews, and accepted of the multitude of his brethren, seeking the wealth of his people, and speaking peace to all his seed."(KJV)*** There is no justice like God's justice! The Bible says one can chase a thousand and two can put ten thousand to flight. How? By being willing to add the seven virtues to our faith and build upon them. Esther did chase a thousand and so can we! You may not ***think so***, but the time will come when you will ***know so!*** The courage of one woman....

"Great is Thy faithfulness!"
"Great is Thy faithfulness!"
"Morning by morning new mercies I see;"
"All I have needed Thy hand hath provided,"
"Great is Thy faithfulness,"
"Lord unto me!"

(Hymn by Thomas O. Chisholm *6)

Author's Comments to the Reader

I never believed that only "saved" or Christian people would be the sole readers of this book. With this in mind, if you are not a Christian but have seriously considered becoming one, I would like to take this time to personally invite you to become a part of God's family. It doesn't matter where you are right now reading these words, the steps to salvation are as simple as the "A, B, C,'s." Sincerity and faith are needed to make the process complete. It only takes a few moments to make the most important decision you will ever make in life, changing it for the better!

First, you must **_Admit_** that you are a sinner in need of a Savior. You realize that you have missed the "mark" by not living according to God's righteous and holy standard. Because of this, you therefore repent of all your sins. Next, you must **_Believe_** that Jesus Christ is the Son of God, that He was born of a virgin, crucified on a cross, and rose from the dead with all power in His hands. Lastly, you must **_Confess_** Jesus as your Lord and Personal Savior, fully committing to live a surrendered, obedient, faithful life to Him. If you've completed these steps, thank Him for saving you. Welcome home! Now ask God to direct you to a Bible believing and Bible teaching church that will further develop and disciple you. Now you may be saying to yourself: **"I don't feel any different, maybe I'm not saved?"** Always remember, being a Christian is not based on *feelings* but on *faith.* You must believe in your heart that you are "saved." Romans 10:9 & 10 states: ***That if thou shalt confess with thy mouth the Lord Jesus, and shalt*** *believe in thine heart that God has raised him from the dead, thou shalt be saved. For with the heart man believeth unto righteousness; and with the mouth confession is made unto salvation."* Don't doubt my friend. Only believe. You are now a child of the King and Heaven belongs to you!

Mary J. Parker

Biography of Mary Parker

Mary Jeanette Parker was born on March 19, 1968 at Mountainside Hospital in Montclair New Jersey. She graduated from Upsala College in 1990 with a B.A. Degree in Business Administration, her concentration being Marketing. While battling a severe case of depression, the Lord spoke to her heart one Saturday night in a way that He had never spoken before. This is how the conversation began: *"If you died tonight, where would your soul rest? In Heaven or Hell?"* She being a morally good person quickly answered **"Heaven?"** To her astonishment she heard. *"No my dear, Hell."* *"You haven't accepted me as your Lord and personal Savior so that makes you a candidate for Hell."* *"You're not bad enough to go to Hell, but you'll never be good enough to go to Heaven without me."* She was converted that night on a city bus while traveling home from work. The very next day (The third Sunday in February 1987), she joined the Faith Temple No. 1 Original Freewill Baptist Church under the leadership of Bishop L. N. Forbes.

Because of her thirst for learning, Mary quickly became a dedicated student of the Bible. The Bible is called "The Good Book" for a reason. Sad to say, the vast majority of people have no idea of the Bible's content or the priceless asset (if given the chance) it can prove to be to mankind. When a person reads its pages and applies the principles to their every day life situations, things around them will dramatically change for the better. Mary hopes that her gifting of making the word of God understandable and relevant to our modern day contemporary culture will encourage others to become students of the greatest book ever written, The Holy Bible. *"O taste and see that the Lord is good: blessed is the man that trusteth in him."* *(Psalm 34:8)*

Bibliography

1. King James Version/Amplified Bible Parallel Edition 1995 (Zondervan)

2. The Bible Knowledge Commentary Old & New Testaments 1983 (Cook Communications Ministries)

3. The King James Bible 1611 (King James I of England)

4. The Life Application/Living Bible 1988 (Tyndale House Publishers)

5. The New Combined Bible Dictionary & Concordance 1961 (C.D. Stampley Enterprises, Inc.)

6. The New National Baptist Hymnal 1977 (Triad Purblications)

7. The Scofield Bible 1909 (Oxford University Press)

8. Webster's Collegiate Dictionary 1981 G. & C. Merriam Co.

9. World Book Dictionary 1981 (Doubleday & Company, Inc.)

10. World Book Encyclopedia 1981 (World Book Childcraft International, Inc.)